LITERACY DEVELOPMENTAL CONT...

ROLE PLAY

12 Sight Vocabulary and Vocabulary Enrichment
- Emphasise commonly used words in the environment, classroom and books. Use these words in games and draw attention to their use in Shared and Guided Reading and Modelled and Shared Writing sessions
- Talk about new vocabulary and use it in a range of contexts

13 Strategies for Word Identification
- Foster phonemic awareness through activities and games involving
  - the identification, segmentation and blending of sounds
  - the recognition, matching and generation of rhymes
- Use personal names to introduce sound/letter relationships and syllabification in play and activities
- Use play and song to teach the alphabet letter names
- Display and use an alphabet frieze
- Construct a class alphabet using children's names. Add other words appropriately, as they are taught
- Draw attention to the relationship between sounds and letters, fostering graphophonic awareness
- Link letters of the alphabet with matching sounds in context
- Use rhyme, rhythm and repetition in texts and games to heighten awareness of relationships between print and sound

14 Vocabulary Extension – Writing
- Talk about interesting words and encourage children to use them in speech and writing

15 Spelling
- Provide models of correctly written words in written responses to children's 'writing'

16 Handwriting
- Teach pencil grip in context

EXPERIMENTA...

11 Editing and Pro...
Teaching is design... with a process they...
- Informally mod... changes to text... ...meaning
- Model simple corrections. Do not expect them to follow suit at this stage

12 Sight Vocabulary and Vocabulary Enrichment
- Introduce simple word recognition activities in context, praising children who recognise a word in a range of contexts
- With the children, build up a bank of interesting and evocative words

13 Strategies for Word Identification
- Continue to work with the class alphabet chart, adding words with the same initial letters
- Teach children to segment words into syllables
- Teach onset and rime through activities and games, stemming from familiar words eg 'I Spy'
- Continue to teach children to use contextual knowledge, patterns of language (syntax), initial letters, blending, onset and rime, sounding out, pictures and sight words to identify words when reading
- Talk about letters and words in context, pointing out distinctive features
- Help children segment words into individual sounds
- Help children represent sounds heard in words with letters written in the order they are heard

14 Vocabulary Extension – Writing
- Frequently refer to and model the use of words from class word banks and classroom print
- Enrich vocabulary through activities such as string writing

15 Spelling
Continue to develop and use all word identification strategies as above
- Model the use of class spelling charts, adding words with similar blends and medial vowels
- Teach children to use word banks, personal dictionaries and familiar books as spelling resources

16 Handwriting
- Teach pencil grip
- Help children understand starting points and direction when formulating letters

...

...ng and Proof...
...del the use of ...
...ple editing ...
...ce children are jointly construct ... beginning proof r...

12 Sight Vocabulary ... Enrichment
- Extend basic sigh... involving childre... games and activi...
- Enrich vocabular... as string writing
- Teach subject spe... measure – maths, ... – literature

13 Strategies for Wor...
- Teach a range of ... strategies, such as ... in big words, usin... sentences to deter... needed to make s... to identify words
- Help children use ... common letter se... rime, word compo... sounding out and ... to identify words

14 Vocabulary Exten...
- Build personal an... focusing on them ... words etc

15 Spelling
- Teach children to ... features of words: ... different sounds, ... different letters
- Continue to build ... to provide a syste... and a record of r...
- Teach children so... strategies, eg Look...

16 Handwriting
- Ensure good penc... poor habits are n...
- Foster clear and fl...
- Help children inte... through handwrit...

INUUM – Major Teaching Emphases

TRANSITIONAL

11 Editing and Proof Reading
- Model the use of proof reading, editing and simple revisions
- Jointly refine and expand proof reading guide to include editing strategies and elements of text revision
- Ensure that children proof read their work after it has been edited

12 Sight Vocabulary and Vocabulary Enrichment
- Discuss and teach subject specific vocabulary and ensure that children can immediately recognise most common words
- Continue to enrich children's vocabularies by searching for evocative and interesting words, and jointly constructing an Interesting Word Chart
- Discuss use of figurative language and technical terms

13 Strategies for Word Identification
- Teach word identification strategies i.e. *use of context, graphophonic knowledge, sounding out, blending, letter and word patterns, sight words, syllabification, segmentation, root words, word components, prefixes, suffixes and morphographs*

14 Vocabulary Extension – Writing
- Continue to add interesting, subject specific and evocative words to word banks

15 Spelling
- Continue to teach visual patterns. Problem solve, construct and chart a list of spelling rules. Make hypotheses and prove/disprove/amend as evidence accumulates
- Introduce Spelling Journal. Teach word-learning strategies. Help children to make up and use mnemonics

16 Handwriting
- Encourage children to take pride in their handwriting
- Encourage experimentation with a range of scripts
- Explore computer graphics and presentation

CONVENTIONAL

11 Editing and Proof Reading
- Model the use of proof reading, editing and revising
- Discuss and evaluate the effective use of the planning, monitoring and revising processes of writing
- Jointly construct an effective Editing Guide
- Editors' marks could be researched and incorporated

12 Sight Vocabulary and Vocabulary Enrichment
- Analyse texts, examining the use of specific words and how they enhance meaning and convey subtle meaning

13 Strategies for Word Identification
- Reflect on the use of a range of word identification strategies, eg *word derivation, roots, components*

14 Vocabulary Extension – Writing
- Continue to extend knowledge of subject specific vocabulary. Extend knowledge of roots, prefixes and suffixes

15 Spelling
- Continue to use Spelling Journal
- Explore word derivation
- Focus on meaning as a guide to spelling
- Teach complex visual patterns such as *scious*, and irregular spellings such as *forfeit* and *quay*
- Continue to problem-solve rules, recording on a jointly constructed chart
- Encourage memory aids such as mnemonics

16 Handwriting
- Help children modify writing to suit purpose, eg *developing speed-writing techniques for note taking*
- Foster development of individual styles, but ensure that focus on decorative script does not disrupt clarity and legibility
- Encourage further exploration and use of computer graphics and modes of presentation

© Education Department of Western Australia

Key Stage One
PRIMARY 1–3

How to assess, plan and teach

Shared and Guided Reading and Writing 1

Shared and Guided Reading and Writing, Key Stage 1
was written by

Alison Dewsbury
Manager, First Steps Consultancy Unit

and

Ross Bindon
Senior Consultant
Education Department of Western Australia

Contents

INTRODUCTION

Modelled, Shared and Guided Reading and Writing	4
How to Use this Book	5

SECTION 1: INTRODUCING *FIRST STEPS*

Literacy Development	7
The Literacy Developmental Continuum	8
Reading and Writing	10
Learning to Read and Write	17
The Management of Reading and Writing in the Classroom	18

SECTION 2: READING

Reading to Pupils	22
Modelled Reading	28
Shared Reading	31
Guided Reading	61
Reciprocal Reading	82
Independent Reading	86

SECTION 3: WRITING

Modelled Writing	88
Shared Writing	93
Guided Writing	98
Paired Writing	100
Independent Writing	107
Lucky Bear and the Writing Bag	112

SECTION 4 CONCLUSION

 SECTION 5 SAMPLE LESSON PLANS

Key Stage 1, Year 1, Term 2   119

APPENDICES

Appendix 1: Scope and Sequence Chart
Appendix 2: Word Identification Strategies

GLOSSARY

BIBLIOGRAPHY

UK BIBLIOGRAPHY

ACKNOWLEDGEMENTS

TITLES IN THIS SERIES

***FIRST STEPS* PROFESSIONAL DEVELOPMENT**

INTRODUCTION

Modelled, Shared and Guided Reading and Writing

Teachers are highly skilled in ensuring that a good balance is maintained between teaching children how to read and write and helping them understand the wider issues involved in reading and writing. In order to do this they employ a range of teaching contexts and strategies designed to provide the right mixture of support, guidance and challenge for their pupils. The spectrum ranges from reading to children and modelling writing, through shared and guided reading and writing, to providing activities to consolidate and extend learning and opportunities for independent work. The aim is to enable children to become independent readers and writers.

In each context the element that needs to be taught becomes the focus of the session, whether this is to elucidate a specific strategy or to demonstrate how to achieve a goal. Contexts are chosen to enable the teacher to modify the amount of support and guidance to meet the needs of the pupil in relation to the demands of the task.

In this book, modelled, shared and guided reading and writing are explained in detail. Although these contexts for literacy teaching are of fundamental importance, they sometimes lack definition. Teachers have said that they do not always know exactly what each involves or how to use each effectively. This book is designed to help teachers decide why it may be more appropriate to use one strategy rather than another to achieve a specific objective. It is also designed to demonstrate the natural links between reading and writing and to emphasise the links between the processes by which they are taught – modelled, shared and guided reading and writing.

Introduction

Teaching contexts are labelled, defined and described in this book to enable teachers to see how and when each can be employed to meet the literacy needs of children and the demands of the curriculum. There is no implication that one context is exclusive of others. Each process informs and supports the others. Modelling and guidance are an integral part of an effective shared reading session, just as sharing is part of modelled and guided reading. The intention of the names is first to identify the context as one that has discernible structure and features, and second, to indicate the most appropriate teaching emphases for each particular context. Which context to use, when and how is ultimately a professional decision for the teacher. Uppermost in the teacher's mind will be these three questions:

- Where are my pupils now? That is, in terms of reading and writing development, what can my pupils currently do? The *First Steps* Literacy Developmental Continuum provides Indicators that can be used to map the progress of pupils as they move along their pathway of development in each element of reading and writing.

- Where do they need to go? The National Literacy Strategy outlines a summary of the range of work and a programme of teaching objectives for each year level of Key Stage 1.

- How will they get there? The Major Teaching Emphases linked to the Indicators of the *First Steps* Literacy Developmental Continuum supply explicit direction for teaching. These Major Teaching Emphases are carefully designed to help pupils move from where they are to where they need to be. It is one thing to know what to teach, another how to teach it. The teaching contexts described in this book provide teachers with ways and means of teaching language and literacy effectively in context.

How to Use this Book

This book has been written as a reference for teachers. It is suggested that teachers use the *First Steps* Developmental Continuum to assess where their pupils are in terms of reading and writing development. Having made a prediction and collected data to confirm that prediction, teachers can use the teaching objectives of the National Literacy Strategy to begin long-term planning. As part of that planning, it will be necessary to select appropriate contexts to teach the objectives of the programme. The purpose of this book is to describe and explain how to use the powerful literacy teaching contexts of modelled, shared and guided reading and writing effectively, so that teachers will be able to choose the most appropriate context for the objectives they have selected.

The following page contains a table that defines these contexts. The table also demonstrates that the contexts can be used to bring about a natural progression from teacher control to pupil independence, which is the ultimate goal of teaching.

Introduction

CONTEXT	Reading to Pupils	Modelled Reading	Shared Reading	Guided Reading	Paired Reading	Performance Reading	Independent Reading
What sort of reading is it?	Reading to pupils	Reading for pupils	Reading with pupils	Reading with pupils	Reading with peers	Reading aloud alone	Reading silently alone
Who reads?	Teacher	Teacher	Teacher and pupil	Teacher and pupil	Pupil	Pupil	Pupil
Who is involved?	Whole class	Whole class / Small group	Whole class	Small group	Pairs	Small group / Individual	Individual
What is the focus?	Enjoyment / Listening / Comprehension	Enjoyment / Word recognition & comprehension strategies	Enjoyment / Word recognition & comprehension strategies	Enjoyment / Comprehension strategies	Enjoyment / Oral reading – fluency	Enjoyment / Oral reading – fluency and expression	Enjoyment / Comprehension
What happens?	Teacher reads aloud / Pupils listen / Discussion limited	Teacher reads aloud / Teacher models strategies	Teacher and pupils read aloud / Discussion about strategies	Teacher directs / Pupils read silently and aloud to substantiate / Discussion	Proficient reader leads reading (aloud) / Learner reads aloud	Pupil reads aloud to inform or entertain	Pupil reads silently to be informed or entertained

SUPPORT ⟶ INDEPENDENCE

CONTEXT	Writing to Pupils	Modelled Writing	Shared Writing	Guided Writing	Paired Writing	Writing for Publication	Independent Writing
What sort of writing is it?	Writing to pupils	Writing for pupils	Writing with pupils	Writing with pupils	Writing with peers	Writing for publication	Writing alone for self or audience
Who writes?	Teacher	Teacher	Teacher and pupil	Teacher and pupil	Pupil	Pupil	Pupil
Who is involved?	Whole class / Individuals	Whole class / Small group	Whole class	Small group / Individuals	Pairs	Small group / Individual	Individual
What is the focus?	Enjoyment / Conveying a message / Feedback	Enjoyment / Processes / Text types / Conventions	Enjoyment / Processes / Text types / Conventions	Enjoyment / Writing process	Enjoyment / Writing fluency	Enjoyment / Purpose and audience	Enjoyment / Purpose and audience
What happens?	Teacher writes / Pupils read	Teacher writes & models strategies	Teacher and pupils write / Discussion about strategies	Teacher directs / Pupils write / Discussion	Proficient writer & learner take turns discussing, dictating & writing	Pupil writes to inform or entertain the public	Pupil writes for a purpose

INTRODUCING *FIRST STEPS*

Literacy Development

Literacy development starts when parents talk, sing and read to their babies. These are good experiences that set the scene for all that is to follow. Babies soon learn to play with books, imitating adults reading and enjoying the bright pictures as they turn the pages. Later on toddlers start to scribble, imitating adults writing. It is through interacting with readers and writers and by the role-playing of reading and writing that young children construct early understandings about the relationships between the spoken and written word. From these early beginnings spring all the exciting adventures with print that follow.

Some children may not have had access to literacy experiences at home, although they may have had many other rich cultural and social experiences. It is crucial that when these children come to school, they are given every possible opportunity to:

- observe readers and writers at work
- interact with books
- take part in 'real' reading and writing experiences.

This will enable them to build the solid foundations that are essential to success in literacy learning.

From early childhood to old age, the ways in which readers and writers develop is driven by their reading and writing experiences and the understandings that grow out of these experiences. Many perceptions about reading and writing emerge from what children see expert readers and writers doing. This is why teachers need to provide clear models of reading and writing in context. Children learn to adapt their literacy behaviours to meet the demands of the classroom. Their literacy growth is shaped by what they believe their teacher values. The specific teaching of literacy understandings and skills needs to be set within and drawn from a context of real reading and writing, so that children have a balanced and realistic view of literacy learning.

A brief overview of spelling development shows how children's experiences shape their perceptions and how their perceptions influence their spelling behaviours. Young children know that print is important and that it is different from pictures, so they produce scribble that looks like writing. Chinese children's scribble emulates the characters of Mandarin, whereas English-speaking children's scribble is based on the writing they see their parents doing. A major breakthrough occurs when children understand that speech is made up of words and English-speaking children realise that a letter or letters can represent the main sound of a word. At this point their writing often consists of a string of letters, each one or two representing the most significant sounds of the words they are writing. The next step occurs when they realise that words can be segmented into a series of sounds and that a letter or letters can represent each sound. This understanding leads them to 'sound-out' every sound they can hear, so *umpire* becomes *umpiyer* and *next* becomes *necst*. Later on, children realise that English spelling is governed by other factors such as acceptable letter patterns, morphemes, meaning and specific rules, so their spelling gradually becomes more conventional.

At every phase of their journey into literacy, readers' and writers' understandings and resultant behaviours are shaped and formed by the experiences they undergo and the teaching they experience. Teachers who know 'where pupils are' on their journey can provide the explicit teaching that is needed at each phase of development across the elements of reading and writing. Teachers need to mix the support and encouragement they offer with an appropriate amount of challenge, so that pupils are constantly moving forward as they reach out towards the next goal. There is always another target to work towards on the lifelong journey into literacy.

The Literacy Developmental Continuum

The Literacy Developmental Continuum, which can be found at the beginning of this book, describes reading and writing behaviours that may be observed as literacy understandings and skills gradually develop. These behaviours are linked, through Major Teaching Emphases, to teaching strategies and activities designed to help pupils make sound progress. The teaching activities and strategies are set out in detail in the *First Steps* books *Word and Sentence Work at Key Stages 1 and 2*, *Fiction and Poetry at Key Stages 1 and 2*, and *Information Texts at Key Stages 1 and 2*. This book deals with the main contexts in which the understandings, strategies and skills of literacy are taught and learned – modelled, shared and guided reading and writing.

The Literacy Developmental Continuum as a Diagnostic Tool

Teachers can use the Literacy Developmental Continuum as a diagnostic tool to enable them to identify what their pupils are achieving in each element of the strands of reading and writing. The descriptions of phases provide thumbnail sketches of the overall progress made by readers and writers. A teacher uses these to gain a general idea of 'where a child is' before matching what the child is doing with 'Indicators', or specific descriptions of literacy behaviours in each listed element of reading and writing. A child's profile may range across two or three phases when each element is considered in detail. Elements have been organised under the categories of Word, Sentence and Text Levels, and the sub-categories of reading and writing.

Teachers may find that some pupils leap ahead in reading, but may not make such good progress in writing and/or spelling. Others may have extremely well developed understanding and skills at the Text Level, but may not be so well advanced at the Sentence or Word Levels, or vice versa. This is quite normal – the important thing is that an accurate profile of each child can be obtained so that the teaching programme can be designed to support each child appropriately by placing children in groups designed to cater for their specific needs.

If more diagnostic detail is required about individual children who may be experiencing difficulties, this information can be found in the pages of Expanded Indicators, which are included as an Appendix in the *Literacy Developmental Continuum* book.

Major Teaching Emphases

Having placed a child on the Continuum by marking Indicators across a range of elements, it is easy to move to the corresponding Major Teaching Emphases. The main purpose of the Continuum is to enable teachers to make direct links between the phase a child has reached in each element and the appropriate teaching strategies. The Major Teaching Emphases outline what needs to be taught to ensure that children make steady progress. Practical strategies and activities that support the Major Teaching Emphases are outlined in the other books in this series. The linking of assessment to teaching enables children to make sustained progress and achieve the objectives of the curriculum.

Use of the Continuum also makes it very easy to differentiate and group children appropriately when they are participating in activities in a Literacy Hour or in other English lessons.

The purpose of the Literacy Developmental Continuum is to enable teachers to:

- identify 'where children are' in the development of their understandings and skills;
- group children appropriately according to need;
- link this assessment with teaching strategies and activities designed to provide the right amount of support and challenge that will enable pupils to make sustained progress;
- monitor children's progress in the course of day-to-day classroom teaching;
- ensure that pupils achieve the targets set for them by the school and the National Literacy Strategy.

A standardised or other test only offers a partial picture of a child's current understandings because it may not take into account different cultural, linguistic or community backgrounds. Observing what children do and say when they are engaged in meaningful tasks enables an accurate and sensitive assessment to be made. This informs the teaching plan so that the actual needs of children can be met appropriately.

Reading and Writing

Reading and writing are complex processes, the elements of which can be classified and grouped in many different ways. The National Literacy Strategy Framework provides an easily accessible way of looking at the teaching of literacy. It organises the teaching of reading and writing within the framework of Word, Sentence and Text Level understandings and skills, at each term and year level. This provides guidance about what are considered to be vital components of classroom learning.

However good a framework may be, it is difficult to capture on paper the essential nature of the integrated, recursive and cyclical processes of reading and writing. It is easy to fragment a complex process into a series of discrete skills. Teachers need to be sure that 'real' reading and writing are modelled and shared with children before individual elements are extracted and taught. If a literacy lesson starts with modelled or shared reading or writing, the danger of presenting these processes to children as a series of discrete components is overcome. Children can see how each element fits into and informs the whole process before concentrating on a single element, such as phonics or spelling, in isolation. It is important to base literacy teaching on contexts that enable children to see the integration of elements within the whole process.

Children need to understand that readers and writers constantly call on one aspect of knowledge, skill and understanding to inform and support another. Although, for instance, grammar has been classified at the Sentence Level, knowledge of grammar is actually necessary at all levels of reading and writing. Other elements, such as topic knowledge, knowledge of the world and society and the ability to think critically are equally important and also impinge on each level of literacy. A teacher's task is to help children integrate Word, Sentence and Text Level understandings and skills. The contexts of modelled, shared and guided reading and writing enable teachers to accomplish this task effectively.

Reading

Sometimes readers are aware of the understandings and skills they are using to gain meaning from a text, but often they apply their knowledge without conscious thought. At the Word Level, the more children are able to read without stopping to struggle with word identification, the more fluent their reading becomes. At the Sentence Level, the more they are able to use their natural knowledge of grammar to bring meaning and coherence to a text, the better their comprehension.

At the Text Level, knowledge of text structure and language appropriate to a specific text form also greatly assists comprehension. It also includes all the 'big picture' elements of reading. These elements are not only contained within a text, but also include all the perceptions and understandings that a reader brings to a text. Factors such as a reader's linguistic, cultural and social background and knowledge of the world have a direct impact on the comprehension and interpretation of text, as does knowledge of the topic, text structure and specific linguistic features. Comprehension and critical response is based on a growing understanding of the world and society. An ability to monitor comprehension automatically at all levels, and use an appropriate strategy when a problem is encountered is the mark of a mature and competent reader.

The following table summarises the Word, Sentence and Text Level model of reading. It is not Key Stage specific.

Word, Sentence and Text Level understandings are used interactively, not sequentially. Each supports and informs the others.	Readers use the following understandings to help them identify and give meaning to print. The most effective contexts for fostering these understandings are modelled, shared and guided reading and writing sessions.
WORD LEVEL UNDERSTANDINGS AND SKILLS *Before children learn to read, they focus on the meaning of a text. They gain meaning from listening to a story and looking at pictures, not on printed words. Later on, when they are learning to read, they focus so heavily on the need to identify the words that meaning can be lost. Expert readers use their awareness and understanding of words automatically. It is only when encountering difficult text that relevant knowledge is brought to the forefront of the mind.*	• **Phonological awareness** – *children who seem to lack this awareness often develop it most easily when they can concurrently see, hear and say a word.* • **Understandings about print** – *these range from the fundamental matching of a spoken to a written word to the concept of directionality.* • **Graphophonic awareness** – *this includes letter/sound relationships and the blending, adding and substituting of sounds and letters.* • **Visual awareness** – *this includes both the automatic recognition of high frequency and other words and the recognition of letter-patterns within words.* • **Awareness of meaning** – *this includes an understanding of morphemes, word components and root words.* • **Grammatical awareness** – *although this would appear to be a Sentence Level element, an understanding of the function of words is an essential component of word identification.*
SENTENCE LEVEL UNDERSTANDINGS AND SKILLS *A young reader uses understandings about spoken language to make sense of written sentences. This involves an awareness of grammar that can not yet be articulated. Children need to develop a 'sense of sentence' and a fundamental understanding of what words are and what they do long before they are overtly taught grammar.*	• **Awareness of meaning within a sentence** – *this includes an understanding of the function of words and the ways in which they work together to make meaning. This helps children identify words in a text as well as comprehend their meaning in a sentence.* • **Awareness of meaning between sentences** – *this is essential for readers' comprehension of a paragraph.* • **Awareness of meaning between paragraphs** – *this provides the key to the logical flow of meaning throughout a text.* • **Awareness of the role of punctuation** – *this is an essential factor in the construction of meaning.*
TEXT LEVEL UNDERSTANDINGS AND SKILLS *Young children come to school with well-established understandings relating to their own home, community and culture. It is on these foundations that comprehension is built. Gradually horizons are extended to include the values and customs of other homes, communities and cultures. Experience and maturity enable readers to construct deeper and wider interpretations of text.*	• **Awareness of strategies readers need to decode text** • **Awareness of comprehension strategies** • **Awareness of strategies involving critical thinking and reader response** • **Awareness of strategies needed for accessing, organising, recording and retrieving information** • **Awareness of the subject of a text** – *a reader needs to approach a text with a conscious awareness of existing knowledge about the topic. It can also help to have some knowledge about the probable values of the author.* • **Awareness of the text structure and linguistic features of a text** – *when reading fiction and non-fiction, an understanding of the way in which the text is structured and the ways in which language is likely to be used greatly assists comprehension.* • **Awareness of the world and society** – *a reader brings to any text his or her own understandings about culture, community, relationships and related happenings. The meaning of a text is constructed by readers as they interact with the words and ideas of the author.* • **Ability to reflect** *on self as a reader, on texts and authors in relation to values and perceptions of the world and society.*

Helping Parents Understand the Developmental Nature of Reading

Parents are eager to help their children in any way that they can. Children usually take books home to read to their parents or carers and it is important that this experience is productive and positive. Sometimes adults, remembering their own schooldays, insist on absolute correctness of word identification, which can have an inhibiting effect on children who are striving to use the 'leave a gap and read on, use the meaning and grammar to make sense, and then have another try' technique.

The best solution is to entice parents to attend a reading workshop, when the reading process can be explained and the best methods of helping children modelled and practised. Some of the factors that can be explained to parents are:

- the overall concept of literacy development as it relates to their children;

- the absolute importance of making sure that reading is always fun and a pleasurable experience for adult and child alike;

- the importance of allowing Role Play and Experimental readers to focus on retelling the meaning of a story, and not the accurate decoding of specific words;

- the importance of encouraging free, fluent and enjoyable telling of a story;

- the need for children to use pictures as clues to meaning;

- the need to look through a book, focusing on the title, illustrations etc, before reading commences;

- the fact that when their children become Early readers, they may focus so much on identifying words that their reading will probably be slow and laboured, unless the text is very familiar (they may even lose the meaning, which can be regained through a little informal discussion);

- the need to give children time to solve their word identification problems by themselves and to praise them when they achieve success;

- the need to know when children are really stuck and to provide support so that there is no feeling of failure;

- the need to talk about a story or information text as a fellow reader who has enjoyed it, rather than as an adult who asks questions while already knowing the answers;

- the possibility of joining a library and regularly borrowing books, and allowing children to choose their own books, even if their choices seem too hard (if a chosen book is too hard, they need to read it with their child and talk about what it means);

- the availability of the teacher to talk through problems, offer advice and share triumphs;

- the need for children to see the teacher, their parents and themselves as members of a team who work together and enjoy the experience.

Writing

Like reading, writing is underpinned by many specific understandings, and demands the use of many complex skills, for instance, handwriting, spelling and the application of grammatical knowledge. All these aspects of writing need to be specifically taught through modelled and shared writing followed by supporting activities. Children also need to have many opportunities for repeated practice of these skills in the context of independent writing for an explicit purpose and an identified audience.

It is crucial that young children are given many opportunities to understand what writing is and what it is for. They need to construct early understandings through the role-playing of writing, in response to adult modelling, long before they are able to formulate letters correctly or understand about the structure of words and sentences. Children use play to work out why and how we write, just as they use play to gain understandings about and rehearse other aspects of life.

Children in Key Stage 1 generally write as they speak, using their unconscious knowledge about the order of words and the structure of language. Their knowledge is rudimentary, because just as words slide together in speech and are not marked by clear boundaries, so the flow of speech is not cut up into discrete sentences. It is only when readers encounter written text that underlying elements of language become visible, because words can then be seen as well as heard. A typical early understanding gained by young writers is that a sentence is a chain of words with a capital letter at one end and a full stop at the other. Before they meet sentences in a written form, sentences do not exist for young children.

One of the major understandings that young children need to gain is that their writing has to stand alone if it is to make sense to a reader. A reader may not share the same background or experience as the writer and does not have the advantage of hearing intonation patterns or seeing body language. This means that writers need to include sufficient background information to orient a reader. This is a very difficult thing for young writers to understand, as they often assume that potential readers share their contextual knowledge in the same way that parents, peers and teachers usually do when participating in conversation.

It is through modelled writing that children gain the clearest understanding about the purpose and elements of writing and the need to orientate a reader. Concepts, skills and strategies that have been modelled are then reiterated and consolidated through shared writing before being further practised with support when children participate in guided writing. Opportunities for children to write for real purposes and audiences, both independently and in supported sessions, need to follow the explicit teaching of specific elements. This enables children to use, reintegrate and apply what they have learned so that understandings and skills can be generalised across a range of contexts.

Writers organise their thinking and construct a plan to ensure that their writing achieves its goal. They need to re-read their work constantly to maintain flow and coherence. Young writers are hindered by their constant need to stop and think about how to spell words. The more words they can spell without conscious thought, the better the flow of thought and writing. This is why it is important to encourage children to take risks and 'have a go' at representing words without stress, knowing that corrections can be made later on if necessary.

The ability of a young writer to use a sense of 'what sounds right' in speech is gradually transformed into knowledge of grammar that underpins the writing, editing and refining of a text undertaken by mature writers. Knowledge of text structure and appropriate use of language enables writers to manipulate and present their work to achieve a widely different range of goals. The researching of a topic, extraction of essential information, making of notes and subsequent transformation of the notes into coherent prose, are essential skills that need to form a large part of every writer's armoury. The use of these skills involves the integration of reading and writing at a very high level. The foundations for learning these skills are laid in Key Stage 1 at a very simple level, when children pool their knowledge about a topic and then, with teacher guidance, classify what they know under appropriate headings.

Even when they compose a simple sentence, young writers are being asked to use many different skills. They need to think about what they want to say, find the right words and arrange them appropriately, work out how to represent the words in print and how to formulate the letters. The tax on their working memory is immense. It is no wonder that when they are asked to place a specific focus on one skill, another appears to regress. Only time and practice will enable children to write fluently. Teachers are very conscious of the demands that writing imposes on children and constantly try to ensure that the pleasure and joy derived from writing is maintained as young writers strive to learn their craft.

Writing Understandings and Skills

Word, Sentence and Text Level understandings are used interactively, not sequentially. Each supports and informs the others.	Writers use the following understandings to help them represent their thought in written words and transmit meaning to others. The most effective contexts for fostering these understandings are modelled, shared and guided reading and writing sessions.
WORD LEVEL UNDERSTANDINGS AND SKILLS *Before children learn to write, they simulate adult writing in play. Later on, when they are learning to write, they focus intently on representing the sounds they hear in words with letters, always logically, but not always conventionally. Expert writers use their awareness and understanding of words, spelling and grammar automatically. Even they, however, constantly need to revise, rethink and rewrite. It is crucial that the joy of writing is not lost in the struggle for perfection.*	• **Phonological awareness** – children develop this most easily when they can concurrently see, hear and say a word. • **Understandings about print** – concepts and conventions; these range from the fundamental matching of a spoken to a written word to the concept of directionality. • **Graphophonic awareness** – this includes letter/sound relationships and the blending, adding and substituting of sounds and letters. • **Spelling** – this includes the acquisition of an ever-increasing bank of words that can be spelt automatically; the ability to use graphophonic understandings; the gradual construction, through problem-solving in context, of rules that govern spelling; a knowledge of exceptions to the rules. • **Awareness of meaning** – this includes an understanding of morphemes, syllabification, word components and root words that enables writers to manipulate words effectively. • **Grammatical awareness** – writers need to understand how words relate to each other.
SENTENCE LEVEL UNDERSTANDINGS AND SKILLS *A young writer uses understandings about spoken language to create written sentences. This involves an awareness of grammar that can not yet be articulated. Children need to develop a 'sense of sentence' and a fundamental understanding of what words are and what they do long before they are overtly taught grammar.*	• **Awareness of the fundamental structure of a sentence** – this includes an understanding of word function, the way words are ordered and the changes they undergo to give them explicit meaning, e.g. changes of tense, voice or person in verbs. Children have some understanding of these factors because of their oral competency long before they are taught any elements of grammar. Their 'sense of sentence' is fostered through reading, writing and sentence construction and manipulation activities. In Key Stage 1, children only deal with major factors such as subject/verb agreement; noun/pronoun agreement and reasonable consistency of verb tense. • **Awareness of word function** – this forms the foundation for learning about word classes, such as nouns, pronouns, verbs, adjectives, adverbs, prepositions, articles and connectives, most of which takes place in Key Stage 2. • **Awareness of how to link sentences in a paragraph and paragraphs in a text** – this needs to be carefully modelled over a long period of time and is not formally taught in Key Stage 1. • **Awareness of the role of punctuation to enhance meaning** – in Key Stage 1 this involves the use of capital letters, full stops, question marks and commas to separate items in a list.
TEXT LEVEL UNDERSTANDINGS AND SKILLS *Early foundations are laid in Key Stage 1 relating to knowledge of text forms, linguistic features and the strategies writers use to achieve their goals. Young writers need a strong sense of audience and purpose and a good self-image.*	• **Awareness of strategies writers need to convey meaning to readers** – this includes orientation and planning. • **Awareness of strategies needed for accessing, organising, recording, retrieving and transforming information** – these can be modelled and used in a very simple form in Key Stage 1. • **Awareness of text structures and linguistic features** – in Key Stage 1 children become familiar with simple text forms such as greeting cards, lists, recounts, procedures (instructions) and simple letters, reports and stories. • **Ability to reflect positively** on self as a writer.

The National Literacy Strategy Framework sets out sequential objectives at the Word, Sentence and Text Levels for each term of every year level. The writing strand of the Literacy Developmental Continuum provides a framework for the assessment and monitoring of progress towards and achievement of teaching objectives. Linked Major Teaching Emphases offer direct teaching focuses, designed to ensure the further development of elements of writing, providing a means of meeting required objectives. Modelled, shared and guided writing provide excellent vehicles for introducing, extending, consolidating and practising the strategies, skills and understandings needed for effective writing. They also offer contexts in which the integration of these skills is clearly demonstrated. They enable children to see how apparently discrete elements of reading and writing are interwoven.

The overall aim is to teach children to become fluent and expressive writers who can adapt their writing to meet the demands of different audiences and purposes, monitoring their composition effectively, detecting potential hurdles and knowing what steps to take to surmount them.

A Scope and Sequence Chart for the teaching of writing is included as Appendix 1 on page 127. This table illustrates the need to expose young writers to elements of writing for a considerable time before formal teaching is commenced.

Helping Parents Understand the Developmental Nature of Writing

Although parents know that children will take time to learn to read and will not become fluent overnight, they frequently expect and believe that spelling and grammar should be correct from the beginning. They can become deeply concerned if the red pen of a teacher does not meticulously correct children's early writing.

It is helpful if teachers can explain that:

- learning to write is as much a developmental process as learning to read;
- children learn to write by writing;
- they will not get everything right first time round;
- while they are concentrating on one particular aspect of writing, control over others may slip temporarily;
- writers need to take risks if they are to learn effectively – children will become 'safe' spellers and very dull writers if they only attempt things that they know they can do.

Children need specific and explicit teaching of each element of writing and they also need opportunities to apply their developing understandings and skills by writing for specific purposes and audiences. The refinement of skills takes a long time and a great deal of practice. When parents realise how much is involved in the writing process and how well young children tackle the challenges they face, they understand that instant perfection is not possible. They then applaud their children's efforts and give them all the encouragement they need at each phase of their learning journey.

Learning to Read and Write

Many children come to school using the spoken language effectively. This does not mean that they are consciously aware of the language they are using. If they are to become literate they need to be aware of and control specific aspects of language, so that they can use them effectively as readers and writers. To do this they need to be given:

- explicit teaching in the contexts of reading and writing so that they understand where a specific understanding or skill fits as a component of the whole;
- repeated practice of each skill or strategy so that they can control its use;
- opportunities to apply and integrate the skill or strategy as readers and writers.

Some children need very little overt practice, as they read and write independently for pleasure and are constantly using understandings and skills in context. Others need a great deal of repeated teaching and practice before they are able to apply a skill or understanding effectively. It is important that such practice is motivating, because bored children do not make good learners. Shared and guided reading and writing offer stimulating contexts that can make essential practice both challenging and fun.

Although reading and writing are often seen as different faces of the same coin, understandings and skills that readers and writers use are not always automatically transferred from one context to the other. For example, many understandings relating to word identification and spelling seem to be similar, but these understandings need to be specifically taught to children in the context of both reading and writing. Skills need to be deliberately practised many times through relevant activities in small group and individual situations before they become part of children's reading and writing repertoires.

In Key Stage 1, children are learning to read and write. They are establishing the early understandings and skills that form the foundation of their growth and development in literacy. By the time they enter Key Stage 2, some of these skills and understandings will have become automatic and all will undergo further development and refinement as pupils move through the school. Skilled and highly focused teaching enables children to gain increasing competency and confidence as they journey towards maturity as readers and writers.

In Key Stage 1, teachers need to place a major focus on the fundamental concepts and conventions of literacy. However, it is vital that the teaching of the 'nuts and bolts' of literacy does not obscure the joys and satisfaction of reading and writing for each individual. From the earliest years children need to see and hear adults writing and reading, and read and write themselves:

- for pleasure and for self-actualisation;
- to satisfy the need for information and the need to communicate;
- to experience a wide range of purposes and audiences;
- in many contexts and in relation to many different text forms.

If this happens, children's literacy experiences will provide a bottomless well of fulfilment, broadening and enhancing their vision of the world and giving them insights into the power that literacy can bring to them.

The Management of Reading and Writing in the Classroom

The fundamental principle of literacy teaching and learning that needs to be enshrined in classroom management is that of implementing a *whole-part-whole* model.

The *'whole'* experience at the beginning of the session provides an authentic reading or writing context, out of which the teaching focus will be drawn. The *'part'* experience is given when the class then divides into small groups to pursue the objective through a designated activity. Activities are appropriately scaffolded to provide support for differentiated groups of children. It is important that all the groups are working towards the same objective – it is the degree of scaffolded support given to each group that will vary. The groups then come together for the final *'whole'* experience of reflection, when the learning of each group is related back to the initial objective and, as it were, inserted back into the reading or writing process.

Sharing the Objective

The objective of a literacy lesson should always be shared with the children before the lesson begins. The teacher might say, for instance, *'Today we're going to think about the ways in which authors begin and end their stories. First I'll read a story to you, so don't forget to listen very hard for the beginning and the end. After that we'll talk about beginnings and endings of other stories and then see what we can find out for ourselves when we move into groups.'* This particular objective relates to the National Literacy Strategy Framework for Teaching, Year 1, Term 2, Text Level 5. This major objective is shared with the class by the teacher. Related objectives that the teacher has noted, but probably will not share, are Word Level 10 and Sentence Level 6. Children need to understand the main objective but may be overloaded if they are expected to take on subsidiary objectives as well.

It is very important that Text, Sentence and Word Level objectives are complementary and clearly support each other. This results in cohesive teaching and focused learning. Children have a common goal to work towards and to reflect upon. Word, Sentence and Text Level objectives can be framed as one major aim when shared with the children.

Whole Class Experience

It is important that all children in a class share a common experience of reading or writing at the start of a literacy lesson. This may take the form of modelled or shared reading or writing. In the example quoted above, the teacher might read a short traditional fairy story to the children, drawing attention to *Once upon a time...* and *...so they lived happily ever after*. A subsequent lesson might start with a shared writing session, in which children and teacher develop a very simple story and choose an appropriate beginning and ending from the range that has been collected by the children.

After the reading, children discuss beginnings and endings and the teacher constructs two charts, one for story beginnings and one for endings. The sentences used in today's story are charted. Children are asked if they can think of any others and one or two suggestions, perhaps initiated by the teacher, are shared and charted.

Group Work

Children now move into differentiated groups.

- **Group 1** needs the support of extensive scaffolding. These children could be given a selection of books they have read very recently, and asked to re-read the first and last sentences. They are asked to decide which 'beginning' they like best and are told that they will be asked to share this information with the rest of the class in Reflection time.

- **Groups 2 and 3** are given a pile of books from the reading corner or library and asked to read the beginnings and endings and decide which sentences make them want to read on, and why. They note their responses, ready for sharing.

- **Group 4** not only carries out the same task, but is also challenged to think of one or two beginnings of their own.

- The teacher conducts guided reading with one or two designated groups, focusing on the same objective.

Children are expected to work independently. As the tasks have been structured according to group capability, this should not be a problem. If any finish early, which they probably will not, they should know exactly what to do next. In this case, they could choose one of the stories with a beginning that appeals to them and read on quietly.

Reflection Time

The class comes together to share their findings. After examples have been written on the charts, discussion centres on what children have learned about the use of 'story language' in books and how this differs from the language of everyday speech. Plans are made to continue to collect beginnings and endings when reading independently, with the ultimate aim of composing a class story.

Two diagrams illustrating this process are shown below.

The Whole-Part-Whole Model

The whole-part-whole model underpins the teaching of literacy in the classroom. Word, Sentence and Text Level objectives are chosen from the National Literacy Strategy Framework of Teaching Objectives. Choice of objectives is guided by the placement of children on the Literacy Developmental Continuum and the scanning of linked Major Teaching Emphases, in the light of the overall teaching plan.

Objectives chosen at the Word, Sentence and Text Levels are directly related to each other within the context of the text chosen for the modelled, shared and guided reading or writing sessions. The three objectives are shared with the children, both orally and in writing, as a single, cohesive target for the literacy lesson.

```
┌─────────────────────────────────────┐
│ The objective is shared with the    │
│ children. The lesson starts as      │
│ children participate in 'real'      │
│ reading and/or writing through      │
│ MODELLED AND/OR SHARED              │
│ READING OR WRITING                  │
└─────────────────────────────────────┘
```

```
┌──────────────────────────────────────────────────────────┐
│ THE WHOLE CLASS UNDERTAKES AN ACTIVITY THAT STEMS        │
│ FROM THE MODELLED/SHARED READING OR WRITING SESSION      │
│ This could consist of a whole-class activity such as a   │
│ Text Innovation, Physical Word Sort, What Comes Next?    │
│ or a Physical Sentence Construction, Expansion or        │
│ Manipulation exercise. This can be used as a 'dress      │
│ rehearsal' for the small group work that follows. The    │
│ activity is focused on the chosen objective.             │
└──────────────────────────────────────────────────────────┘
```

Guided reading group, working with teacher. Same objective	Scaffolded small group activity. Same objective	Scaffolded small group activity. Same objective	Scaffolded small group activity. Same objective	Scaffolded small group activity. Same objective

```
┌──────────────────────────────────────────────────────────┐
│ Plenary session that integrates the 'part' activities    │
│ back into the whole literacy experience by reflecting    │
│ on the achievement of the objective through both the     │
│ modelled/shared reading/writing and the small group      │
│ activities.                                              │
│ NOTE: Unless the whole class shares the same objective,  │
│ which runs like a thread through the whole lesson, the   │
│ reflection undertaken in the plenary session will be     │
│ meaningless. The plenary session is not intended simply  │
│ as a 'show and tell' episode, although this element may  │
│ be included in it, but as a reflection on the            │
│ achievement towards or achievement of the lesson         │
│ objective.                                               │
└──────────────────────────────────────────────────────────┘
```

© *First Steps:* NLS edition

Content – Animal Study

- Each child in the class is involved in organising information from the same texts – in this instance, descriptions of several animals.
- There are three levels of difficulty in operation.

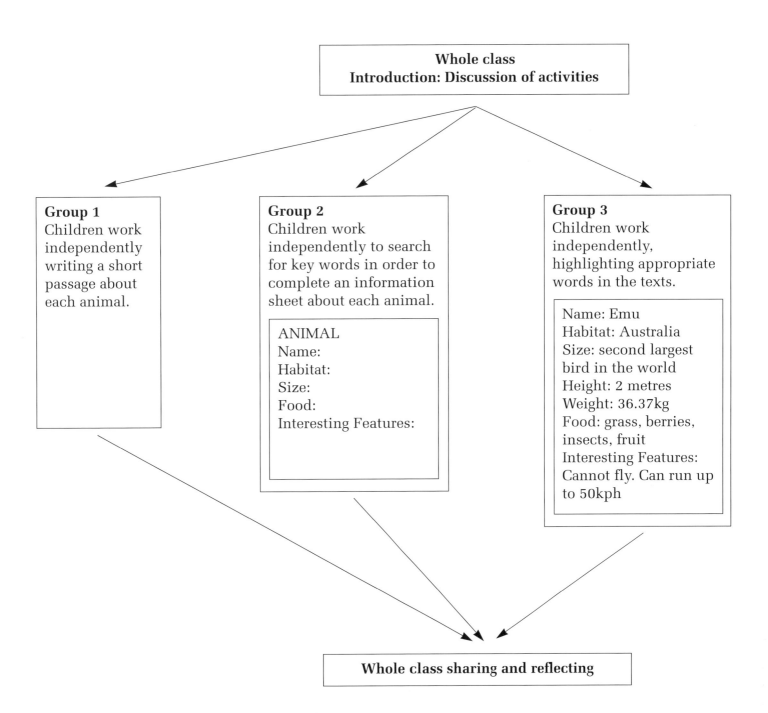

The teacher works with a group conducting guided reading.

READING

Reading to Pupils

Some children come to school from homes where story-telling is one of the routines of family life. Their homes are full of books and they have their own collection of favourite stories. They quote facts from non-fiction texts they have listened to, confidently sharing information about animals, cars, space or dinosaurs. They are familiar with the language of books and see them as a source of pleasure and interest.

Other children bring different experiences to school. Some come from communities with a strong tradition of oral story-telling. Some come from rich cultural backgrounds and have shared in many of the rituals and celebrations that are part of their religious or traditional life. Others have attained an amazing degree of independence.

It is extremely important that, when they come to school, all children are exposed to rich and stimulating literacy experiences so that all can develop similar literacy understandings. Without these experiences and understandings, children experience considerable disadvantage in their school learning. All children need to listen to stories or to fascinating information read from a non-fiction text. For children who are already avid listeners, the continuing experience at school will increase their sense of continuity, belonging and pleasure. For other children, the experience of being a listener will open magic doorways into new worlds.

One of the most important tasks a teacher can undertake is to read aloud to pupils. Reading to children can happen incidentally in a whole range of contexts, such as reading a letter from children from another school, or reading something relevant from a local community newspaper. One of the most important sessions, however, happens at a special time set aside for that purpose, a time that becomes the focal point of the day, to which all children look forward with eager anticipation. At this time a story or interesting information text is read to the class.

When teachers read to children their objective should be to share their pleasure and interest in reading with children. The reading should be uninterrupted and expressive. There should be no strings attached to the session – no questioning, no teaching of strategies, no focus on any of the mechanics of print or process. If discussion erupts spontaneously and children wish to share their perceptions and reactions, then that becomes part of the experience and adds another dimension to it. The purpose of the session is always sheer pleasure. It is to enable the author to speak to the children and the teacher to impart the joy of reading.

Why Read to Pupils?

It is obviously necessary to read books to young pupils who are unable to read them independently. In Nursery and in Reception classes teachers give great importance to the story-reading session, which is conducted simply for pleasure. It is extremely important that the place and purpose of this session is not lost as children move through the school and the need to instruct becomes paramount. The place for instruction is in shared or guided reading sessions, not when children are listening for pleasure. Even after children have become competent readers, listening to a story is still one of the great pleasures of life.

Successful reading teaching is built on the foundation of a love for reading and an understanding of what books can offer in life. If children have already had a glimpse of this, it is important that their understanding is reinforced and deepened. If children have not had the opportunity to develop this understanding, then it is crucial that it is introduced and fostered.

Reading to pupils enables teachers to:

- demonstrate fluent and expressive oral reading
- demonstrate their love for reading
- demonstrate the value of regular reading
- show pupils how a particular text should be read, e.g. non-fiction text selectively, poetry dramatically or with emotion
- whet the reading appetites of pupils by introducing new books and authors
- affirm the value of returning to re-read old favourites.

Reading to children enables pupils to:

- enjoy a text unhindered by any restraints, for example, limited ability to read the text for fear of being questioned afterwards
- comprehend challenging or abstract concepts that might be too difficult for independent reading, but can be mediated through the fluency and expression of the teacher's delivery
- become aware of a range of unfamiliar text forms and vocabulary in context
- broaden their horizons and extend their imagination.

When Do I Read to Pupils?

Teachers read to children at any time, whenever the opportunity arises. However, many choose to set aside a particular time for this special interaction.

It may be a good idea to take 10 or 15 minutes to read to children after lunch or following a playtime. Sometimes teachers like to end the day with a quiet period dedicated to reading a story. The important thing is that children know that their story-time is inviolate. They know it will come and they know when it will come. This can be a saving factor for a restless, overactive child or for one who is having a bad day. Reading to children usually has a calming and soothing effect on them. The focus is no longer on performance or behaviour, so children can relax as they lose themselves in the story.

Reading to children need not be seen as belonging to the preserve of 'English' or 'Literacy'. Teachers may introduce a topic in history or geography by saying, *'I would like to read you the diary of a schoolboy in Alaska...'* or *'I've found a wonderful true story about a father who escaped with his two little girls from a volcano that was erupting in New Zealand. It's very exciting, specially as it was the two girls who saw what was happening and woke their father up.'* In this way the teacher can not only awaken interest in the topic, but can also enable all pupils to approach it with confidence and understanding.

How Do I Choose my Objective?

The objective of reading to children must always be to enjoy the text. In addition to this there will be hidden benefits such as becoming familiar with a different text form or author, or 'exploring' a new country or another person's life. These benefits, however, are always incidental and subordinate to the main purpose of the session. They are not explicitly taught. If there is discussion following the reading, it needs to be led by the children and should never consist of interrogation or requests for explanation. Discussion is likely to encompass talk about feelings or contributions from children who have linked the reading to their own experience.

Are Pupils Grouped?

Usually teachers read aloud to the whole class. Children do not need to see the book; as long as they can hear, they can enter their own world as they listen. There is great value in the fact that everyone has shared the same experience.

How Do I Select Reading Material?

Teachers usually know their pupils very well and are able to judge what they will enjoy best. A story may be chosen because it is funny or will appeal to children from a particular community. A poem may be chosen because it depicts a child or expresses an emotion to which the class can readily relate. An information text may be found that will extend a current interest in, for example, cats, trains or dinosaurs.

Sometimes texts can be found outside the covers of a book. The Internet provides a rich source of interesting texts, as do magazines or community newspapers. Letters, especially those written by an older generation when young, can fascinate children, as can diaries or letters from children in different countries.

It may be a good idea to construct an informal timetable of text forms so that children are given the opportunity to be exposed to a wide range of reading materials.

DAY	MONDAY	TUESDAY	WEDNESDAY	THURSDAY	FRIDAY
Text form or genre	Poetry	Letter or journal	Story	Non-fiction	Teacher- or class-made text

Teachers may prefer to use the reading time to share a longer book and serialise it by reading a chapter a day. Many adults look back with pleasure to their own school days when a beloved teacher read another chapter aloud each day from one of Enid Blyton's *Magic Faraway Tree* books, or one of the *Narnia* series by C.S. Lewis. When children are older, teachers may choose to set aside one day a week for serial reading, but in Key Stage 1 a week can be too long to wait for the next instalment. Young children need to listen to an instalment each day.

When children are young, the range of books that they are able to enjoy independently is invariably limited to picture books, old favourites or very simple repetitive texts. When teachers read to children they are able to share texts that are within children's conceptual capacity, but would be too difficult for them to tackle alone. It is important that the level of difficulty is carefully judged, as although children will cope with more complex material if it is read to them, the flow of the reading should not be interrupted by explanations of difficult words or concepts that may prove to be too challenging.

If the complexity of vocabulary and concept is well judged, children can become familiar with a text form long before the form is formally introduced and taught. This will give them a head start when they encounter the form a year or more down the track. In this way reading to children precedes, enhances and provides the foundation for the shared and guided reading sessions that will follow later on.

Another great source of reading material is the children themselves. Children who have enjoyed or been fascinated by a particular story, poem or informational text, may be delighted to bring it to school for the teacher to read to the class. Children love to have their choices endorsed and affirmed, and other children benefit from and enjoy hearing such texts read aloud. Usually a great deal of animated discussion follows such a session. It is important that children who do not have access to books at home are also given an opportunity to share a favourite book. If a child has no books, the teacher may lend a pupil a book from home as a special treasure, and encourage the child to talk about it and ask to have it read to the class when it is brought back to school.

Children like to be consulted and to feel that they have a stake in what goes on. It may be a good idea to help them fill in a simple questionnaire to guide the choice of books.

```
I like books about:
Animals          ☐
Children like me ☐
People in other countries ☐
Sport            ☐
Adventure        ☐
Facts            ☐
Other things like..................................
```

Children could talk through this survey with the teacher and each other, modifying and adding to it as they wish. They could then either tick chosen items or write a few words, according to their capacity or inclination.

Do I Need to Know the Text Well?

It is usually wise to pre-read materials before reading aloud to children. In Key Stage 1 this is not an arduous task, as texts are simple and may already be well known. Even when this is the case, it may be advisable to refresh the memory so that forgotten stumbling blocks can be identified and circumvented. On one occasion, for instance, a teacher re-discovered a well-loved book that her own mother had read to her as a child. It was J.R.R. Tolkien's *Letters from Father Christmas* (re-published in Collins Children's Books, 1995). It is a most attractive and engaging book with a letter to be extracted from an envelope on every page. Time was short and the teacher was well launched into her reading before she found that the letters, which were written by Tolkien to his children between 1920 and 1937, depicted the bad goblins as being black and having a nasty smell. In those days nobody had realised how much this type of stereotyping could influence attitudes. A quick read-through before school would have left her better prepared to improvise slightly and adjust things to meet today's requirements without losing the essence of the book!

It is also helpful to know if a book makes reference to life situations such as separation or illness. It is often wise to be prepared in case a child has been experiencing a similar problem. It may not be necessary to avoid the reading of such a book, as it may have extremely positive outcomes, but it is as well to be prepared.

It may also be sensible to preview an information text so that rather than reading through an entire text, the most interesting, pertinent or engaging parts can be extracted. If a selection needs to be made, it is good to be well prepared.

It is a good idea to avoid using big books for the teacher's reading time. These books are ideally suited for shared reading sessions, but can be unsuitable for a sustained, fluent reading of a text. The format of only one or two lines of print and a picture to a page can be intrusive in this context.

What Resources Will I Need?

All that is needed is a good book and a class of eager children. The mechanics of the session are a matter of individual choice. Many teachers like to gather the children round in an intimate circle, but others prefer it if children sit quietly at their desks. In some classes 'togetherness' is a good idea, in others it may not be! It is a good idea to remove any potential distractions so that children are free to concentrate and lose themselves in the reading. Some like to shut their eyes so that they can project mental images more easily.

A tape-recording is a poor substitute for an understanding, enthusiastic and warm teacher. It is not recommended that taped stories are used in this valuable read-aloud time. The relationship between the reader and the text needs to be experienced by children, who are quick to recognise involvement and engagement. On the other hand, the use of video can provide a bridge to reading for children unfamiliar with books but extremely at home with television and video.

Sometimes it can be a good idea to invite a guest reader. It is good for children to realise that many adults are avid and dedicated readers who enjoy sharing favourite books and love reading them aloud to others. Two teachers could exchange classes for a short while. Alternatively a parent, a grandparent or a carer may be willing to give a quarter of an hour to such a good cause. It may be possible to persuade a footballer or well-known person from the community to come along. A male role-model can make an immense impact on reluctant boy readers. If another reader is brought into the classroom, this provides the teacher with a wonderful opportunity to model sustained, attentive listening. It is extremely important that the temptation to take the register or review the week's work is resisted.

What is the Role of the Teacher?

The teacher's role is to:

- engage the children's interest
- read the text expressively
- share illustrations and diagrams when appropriate, but not if the text has a picture for each sentence, as the fluency will be lost
- respond succinctly to any relevant questions that are asked, but not to invite such questions as they may distract listeners from the flow of the story or text.

How Does Reading to Children Work?

Children like to know a little about the text before listening to it. A brief introduction could include why the text was chosen, something about the author and whether it is a story or information text. For example, *'I'm going to read you a story about a family that had a new baby. I think we'll enjoy it, because some of you have had new babies in your families, and we all enjoyed meeting Lee's new baby brother yesterday, didn't we?'*

Teachers are good at reading texts fluently and expressively. They know how to pause at just the right moment to express curiosity, surprise, excitement or sorrow. It is important to share these reactions with pupils to let them know that teachers are affected by what they are reading and that this shows that there is a special relationship between an author and a reader. Reading a book can have as great an impact as watching a television programme or seeing a film – or sometimes an even greater impact. Children can even begin to understand that the impact of a book can be greater than that of television, video or film because readers create their own pictures in their heads and do not depend on other people for their interpretation of a story.

Sometimes the reading of a book can flow into an appropriate activity. It is important, however, that this does not happen too often. Children need to love books for their own sake and must not be led to believe that the outcome of reading should always be a flurry of activity or a focus on comprehension. The most important outcome of a reading session is that children learn to value, treasure and enjoy books for themselves and for what they can offer, rather than as springboards for 'school' activities.

Modelled Reading

What is Modelled Reading?

In every culture children watch what adults do. Sometimes they re-create adult actions and interactions in their play. Sometimes they join in with the adults, participating in whatever is going on and faithfully reproducing what they see. An immense amount of teaching and learning takes place in this natural and almost involuntary context. In every sphere of life people learn by watching and working alongside experts. Apprentices accompany proficient workers who become their mentors. A great deal of teaching is carried out on the job. The expert shows how things are done and talks the learner through procedures step by step. Modelling the task that is to be learned and accompanying actions with a running commentary to explain what is going on is probably the most ancient, popular and effective teaching technique in the world.

Modelled reading is the name given to the context in which the explicit and planned demonstration of reading strategies is the prime objective. It involves the teacher reading an enlarged text to a group of children and thinking aloud about the strategies that are being used to recognise words and comprehend meaning. Children participate by listening and watching rather than by contributing, suggesting and pursuing points through discussion.

Why Model Reading Strategies?

While some children learn to read and to integrate and apply a range of reading strategies without explicit teaching, most pupils need direct teaching and specific guidance to help them become proficient readers.

Modelled reading:

- provides explicit demonstrations of reading strategies
- builds children's knowledge about the English language
- shows how reading and writing are related.

When Do I Use Modelled Reading?

Modelled reading is most effective when conducted just before children are expected to use the strategy that has been modelled. The first 10 to 15 minutes of a Literacy Hour is an ideal time to teach a specific reading skill or strategy explicitly. Children can then spend the next period of time actively engaged in using the skill or strategy in the context of an activity, or in a guided reading session.

If a small group of children is experiencing difficulty with a particular aspect of the reading process, they may need special help. The teacher may wish to set the other groups to work for 20 minutes on a familiar activity to allow time to repeat the modelling of the strategy, perhaps using a slightly different context. This additional session need occupy only 10 minutes, so that the group can spend the 10 remaining minutes completing an appropriate follow-up activity.

How Do I Choose my Objective?

Teachers know only too well how much there is that children need to learn and it is tempting to try to address a range of objectives at one time. However, this can be counter-productive, as it is only possible for children to focus on one or two things at once. If the working memory is overloaded, nothing will be achieved. A swimming coach might say, *'Watch how I keep my legs straight as I kick,'* having decided to focus on refining arm movements at another time. If a child can focus on one objective at a time, learning will be effective and the child will not become overwhelmed and confused.

Modelled reading is best used to demonstrate the use of reading strategies to children, as well as to emphasise fluency and expression. Too many Word Level interruptions can fragment listeners' experience of the reading process.

The *First Steps* Literacy Developmental Continuum helps teachers identify where children are in terms of their literacy development in each element of reading and provides a list of Major Teaching Emphases appropriate for each element of development. The list of Termly Objectives published in the National Literacy Strategy Framework provides a structure of progression for the required range of work. It may be appropriate to choose an objective from a previous term, or even year, for children who are experiencing difficulties.

By accessing these two documents and using knowledge of children's current understandings, teachers are able to choose an objective that will meet the needs of their pupils.

In choosing objectives for modelled reading sessions, it will become apparent that some objectives will benefit the entire class, whereas others will be suited specifically to small groups. Modelled reading can be conducted with either the whole class or a small group. Pupils may be grouped together because they all need to learn a particular reading strategy, such as self-monitoring and self-correction. Alternatively, reading groups may have been determined by differentiating groups according to their developmental phase in a particular area.

How Do I Select Reading Material?

Reading material for modelled reading is generally chosen on the basis of the objective to be taught. For instance, the story *I Fell out of Bed* by Miriam Simon and June Goulding (Ginn, 1994) could be used to model the use of pattern and rhyme as a reading strategy. A book such as *The Pizza Princess* by Miriam Simon and Jan Nesbitt (Ginn, 1998) could be used to demonstrate the use of context and a predictable language pattern. An informational text such as *Humpback Whales* by Anna Kyjak (Ginn, 1998) could be used to illustrate an author's device such as a question-and-answer technique.

Text needs to be enlarged for the purposes of modelled reading, so that teachers can point to words and sentences as they explain the reading strategies they are using. Big books are ideal for this purpose, but text, such as a recount of a class event, written on a large sheet of paper is also very suitable. The text should be slightly more difficult than that which children can read independently. Teacher intuition is usually a good guide to the required level of difficulty, but if a formula is required the one often quoted is that children should not have difficulty with more than one word in ten.

Do I Need to Know the Text Well?

It is essential that teachers pre-read the material to be used in a modelled reading session. As the choice of text is determined by the objective to be taught, this means that the book will have been carefully chosen in advance to make sure that the text lends itself to the teaching of a specific strategy. The teaching points of the lesson need to be planned in conjunction with the text. If, for instance, the objective of the lesson is to teach children how punctuation helps a reader to make sense of the text and to read fluently, a text need to be chosen with this in mind. It is no good choosing a text that continually uses one sentence to a line, so that the full stop is always at the end of a line of print. This can confuse children, who may draw the conclusion that a sentence always occupies one line of print. It is amazing how many big books are written in this way! A book like *The Flying Turtle* by Gill Munton and Stephen Holmes (Ginn, 1998) offers a simple text with many good teaching opportunities relating to punctuation. The teacher would help children notice how the intonation pattern of reader's voice is guided by the sentence boundaries, and how, in this book, commas are used to show smaller units of meaning within a sentence.

What Resources Will I Need?

A successful modelled reading session simply requires an enlarged text, a willing teacher and a focused group of children! A sturdy easel to hold the book frees the teacher to use a pointer when referring to words, illustrations, punctuation and other text features. A store of Post-it stickers can be useful in case it is necessary to cover over a word or part of a word to illustrate a point. For instance, to show how a long word can sometimes be broken into two parts to make it easier to read, one part of a compound word could be covered over.

> They kicked the ☐ ball as hard as they could.

In modelled reading, the teacher's role is one of:

- engaging pupils' interest
- reading the text aloud expressively
- thinking aloud about the targeted skill or strategy (objective)
- demonstrating how readers make sense of print.

How Does Modelled Reading Work?

Before Reading

The teacher explains why the text was chosen and what strategy or skill will be taught. For example, *'I want to read you a book called* The Flying Turtle, *by Gill Munton and Stephen Holmes. I was really pleased when I found the book, because the story comes from the Caribbean, which is where Lee comes from, so he can tell us much more about it afterwards. Also I would like you to see how the author has used speech marks to tell us when someone is speaking.'*

During the Reading

The teacher demonstrates fluency and expression, pausing at predetermined places in the text to demonstrate the skill or strategy that is the focus of the session. If the objective to be taught was self-correction, the thinking aloud might sound like this: *'Peter struggled to lose the rope from the dog's neck...Wait a moment, that doesn't make sense – he couldn't **lose** the rope, he's trying to get it undone, I'll read it again...Peter struggled to loose the rope from the dog's neck...That's right, that makes sense now...The dog whimpered, as if it knew Peter was trying to help.'*

Although children can ask questions if they wish to, the teacher is in control of the session, as the aim is to give repeated, explicit demonstrations of when, how and why particular skills and strategies are used by effective readers.

After Reading

It is important that a review of the objective is undertaken after the reading. The goal of the session should be reiterated and children asked if they now feel that they understand what has been taught and if they will be able to start using the skill or strategy themselves. If the thinking aloud has been clearly understood by the children, their responses will reflect their new understanding. It may be that it is necessary to revisit a section of the text or choose a different text to illustrate the same point.

It is extremely important that, as soon as possible after the session, pupils can take part in activities or in a guided reading session so that they can immediately use and practise what they have learned. The Literacy Hour lends itself to this teaching/learning/practising structure. At the conclusion of the hour, after children have had the opportunity to try out and practise a skill or strategy in differentiated groups, all come together for further reflection on what has been learned.

Shared Reading

What is Shared Reading?

The context of shared reading is powerful and versatile, enabling children to share in the reading process with a skilled reader. It is the classroom version of a bedtime story – warm, interactive and fun. The teacher and children gather round a big book and read aloud with enthusiasm and verve. It is a co-operative and supportive opportunity for children to enjoy a shared text on a daily basis.

Although shared reading has appeared in many forms, there are characteristics by which it can be readily identified. In shared reading:

- children work in large, mixed ability groups or whole classes; although whole-class work is common, it is important to be sure that children at the back or on the fringes of the group are not inadvertently excluded

- children sit comfortably within sight of an enlarged text; this is often a big book, but materials such as posters, enlarged magazine or newspaper articles, poems or hand-written pieces can also be used

- discussion about the text, including layout, illustrations, language use and vocabulary is ongoing

- a fluent and expressive reading by the teacher may precede the whole class reading
- the initial reading of a text should be uninterrupted and should focus on meaning and enjoyment
- the teacher enthusiastically leads the class in oral reading, but may provide opportunities for individual or choral reading
- sessions are generally planned in a sequence, involving re-reading for different purposes on each subsequent occasion
- sessions are short and focused (about 15 minutes).

In shared reading sessions, children are encouraged to make personal links to the text and offer interpretations that reflect their cultural and linguistic backgrounds. These contributions provide an excellent preparation for teaching that a reader makes a major contribution to meaning within a text and that meaning is not only dependent on the author.

The group is also able to tackle the challenges of the reading process by listening to the teacher talking about the text and what a reader does to make meaning, as well as sharing knowledge about their own reading processes and understandings of the particular text form.

The managed blend of explicit teacher-modelling, choral reading and focused discussion is what makes shared reading an excellent strategy for supporting pupils from a range of cultural, social and linguistic backgrounds.

Shared reading enables pupils to:

- access and enjoy a text that may be slightly beyond their independent reading level
- increase fluency through the supported re-reading of a text
- test their theories about reading in a safe and supportive forum
- consolidate a sight vocabulary and knowledge of sound/letter relationships in an authentic context
- gain an insight into the decoding and comprehension strategies employed by able readers.

Shared reading enables teachers to:

- demonstrate on a daily basis that reading is meaningful and pleasurable
- introduce the whole class to a content focus, text feature or reading strategy
- model skills and strategies used by effective readers
- support weaker readers in their comprehension of difficult text
- observe the range of reading understandings and strategies used by pupils.

When Do I Use Shared Reading?

Within the Literacy Hour, shared reading provides an effective springboard for a whole class teaching focus that may be refined or extended when working with a smaller group and consolidated through extended practice in related activities. It is an extremely practical teaching strategy, providing a common starting point for a variety of subsequent activities that can be scaffolded so that children can participate in them with varying degrees of support, according to need. Shared reading is best used at the beginning of the Literacy Hour to provide a common class focus for the teaching of appropriate objectives, with more specific whole class and small group work to follow.

Beyond the Literacy Hour, shared reading can be used to introduce or extend a unit of work in another subject area such as geography, history or science. Teachers are able to provide support for pupils as they contend with a new concept or with vocabulary that may be strange to them, and pupils are able to support each other as they talk about and share interpretations of the text and ways of tackling new words. If a topic is introduced by means of shared reading, the class has a common source of information and a shared springboard for discussion and activities.

A shared reading session can provide a wonderful forum for helping children to understand that different people can respond in different ways to the same text. For example, children can react in a whole range of ways to the same poem or story. Their family and cultural experiences influence children's responses to a text. Sometimes children are able to understand that different perceptions of a person or event can be equally valid, but very often they feel strongly that their own interpretation must be right. The context of shared reading exposes pupils to the idea that there is more than one way of looking at things and that the perceptions of others can be as valid as their own.

Shared reading is also an excellent way of introducing pupils to some of the ways that information is transmitted in texts. Pictures sometimes carry as much information as words in a story. For example, in the book *Handa's Surprise* by Eileen Browne (Walker Books, 1994), Handa has gathered seven pieces of fruit to take to her friend Akeyo. She carries the fruit in a basket on her head. On the way to her friend's village, one animal after another steals a piece of fruit, so that by the time Handa is nearly there, the basket is empty. Fortunately a runaway goat butts a tangerine tree just as Handa is walking underneath and the basket fills up with tangerines. In this book the pictures carry the story line. Without them the words would make no sense at all. This is a brilliant book to teach children to use picture cues effectively. It also helps children to see that illustrations can provide just as much information as words and that pictures often move a reader far beyond the confines of a text.

Shared reading can be used to introduce children in Key Stage 1 to simple graphs, diagrams and tables in non-fiction texts. In a supportive environment children learn how to interpret these devices and how they extend the reader's understanding of a text.

The worth of shared reading sessions is maximised when teachers are able to take advantage of the links between literacy skills and subject area knowledge that needs to be learned. These links help pupils to generalise their literacy understandings and skills and use them to good effect in a whole range of different contexts.

How Do I Choose my Session Objectives?

Almost all Text Level, Sentence Level and Word Level objectives can be taught through shared reading. As in modelled reading, it is crucial that children are not expected to focus on too many things at once. However, it is often possible to combine objectives at the Word, Sentence and Text Levels in such a way that one objective supports and complements another. This does not over-tax children's working memories and allows a smooth flow of teaching to take place throughout the Literacy Hour. For instance, the objectives chosen for a Literacy Hour might be to teach children that a specific vowel phoneme, such as *ea,* can represent a variety of sounds, and to use knowledge of sentence structure to help with the identification of a word containing the *ea* phoneme, by using the read-on/read-back strategy to find out which 'sounding' of an *ea* word is appropriate in context.

Children would participate in the reading of a text that featured a variety of *ea* words and would learn to identify them using the read-back/read-on strategy. After the reading, children would identify words containing *ea* in the text and classify them according to sound. The class could then divide into groups, four of which might take part in Word Sort activities focusing on this element. A fifth group might participate in guided reading with the teacher, using a different text that also featured the vowel phoneme, gaining practice in the use of the new reading strategy to identify the words.

When the whole class is gathered together for reflection time at the end of the hour, they could discuss what they had learned about the vowel digraph and how the read-back/read-on strategy had helped them and how they could use the strategy when they were reading independently. The vital factor is that every child has a shared objective to discuss.

The following example shows how the Literacy Developmental Continuum and the linked Major Teaching Emphasis can be used in conjunction with the National Literacy Strategy Programme of Teaching Objectives to choose an objective.

- *Literacy Developmental Continuum:* Early Phase Indicator 13 – uses some knowledge of word identification strategies including knowledge of the topic; pictorial cues; grammar; sounding-out and blending; onset/rime; and simple letter patterns, e.g. *ing*

- *Literacy Developmental Continuum:* Early Phase Major Teaching Emphasis 13 – teach a range of word identification strategies... Help children use visual patterns, common letter sequences, onset/rime...

- *National Literacy Strategy:* Year 2, Term 3, Text Level 2 – use phonological, contextual, grammatical and graphic knowledge...

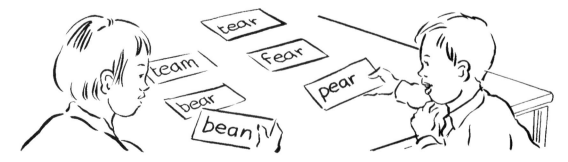

The next example shows how a subsequent grouping of objectives would provide further consolidation of the reading strategy the children were learning by extending focus to include common words that they need to add to their vocabulary of words they can recognise on sight:

- *Literacy Developmental Continuum:* Experimental Phase Indicator 1 – matches some spoken words with written words when reading a book or environmental print; Experimental Phase Indicator 12 – recognises personally significant words in context; Experimental Phase Indicator 14 – uses a small bank of known sight words

- *Literacy Developmental Continuum:* Experimental Phase Major Teaching Emphasis 1 – model and explain reading strategies such as rereading, reading on, self-monitoring and self-reflection in context... provide opportunities for children to read aloud material that is predictable, familiar and contains natural repetition; Experimental Phase Major Teaching Emphasis 12 – informally model how an author makes changes to text to enhance meaning

- *National Literacy Strategy:* Year 1, Term 1, Text Level 1 – to reinforce and apply their word-level skills through shared and guided reading, to use phonological, contextual, grammatical and graphic knowledge to work out, predict and check the meanings of unfamiliar words and to make sense of what they read; Sentence Level 1 – to expect written text to make sense and to check for sense if it does not; Sentence Level 2 – to use awareness of the grammar of a sentence to decipher new or unfamiliar words, e.g. predict text from the grammar, read on, leave a gap and re-read; Word Level 9 – to read on sight approximately 30 high frequency words; Word Level 7 – for guided reading, to read on sight high frequency words specific to graded books matched to the abilities of reading groups

By grouping objectives in this way, objectives at the Word, Sentence and Text Levels are targeted, but children are only asked to focus on one operation, using a specific context. It is always wise to follow the same objectives through each section of a Literacy Hour so that the children's learning experience is coherent, cohesive and able to be jointly reflected upon at the end of the session.

Many objectives, such as reading for different purposes and becoming aware of a range of text features or aspects of language use, are achieved by engaging children in the reading of a variety of texts over an extended period of time. Others, like drawing information from the cover, the title and the pictures before reading a text, can be accomplished by adopting a routine set of reading strategies (see Discussion Guide on page 55). One Head Teacher took over a Year 1 class in an emergency. She was delighted when a small girl, politely interrupting as she started to read a story, said, *'Excuse me, Mrs Baker, but we **always** talk about the title and the cover and the pictures before we start to read!'* Although these general objectives are important, they are rarely the focus of the session. Careful planning of the use of a variety of text forms and regular use of guiding comments and questions will ensure, over time, that they are achieved.

The more directly and explicitly the teacher shares the chosen objectives with the children the better. Many teachers tell the children exactly what the objectives for the session are at the beginning of the Literacy Hour. They may do this before the initial reading of the text for pleasure, or may choose to share the objective with the children once the first reading is over and the children are ready to study the text in detail. For instance, *'Today we are going to talk about the words that rhyme in this poem and see if they are all spelt in the same way. When we've done that we'll have some fun making up our own poem like this one and finding some of our own words that rhyme.'*

It is often a good idea to write down the objective and pin it up where everyone can see it. Then, at intervals during the lesson, the objective is reiterated so that children do not lose their focus. *'Well, now we've found all the words that rhyme and written them down on cards. Do you remember that we said we'd see if they were all spelt the same? What do you think? Let's try to put the rhyming words into groups that are spelt the same way.'*

When an objective has been shared with the children it is important that they can see how it is being achieved and are not distracted by red herrings. If the focus is on rhyming words, the teacher resists the temptation to pursue discussion about directionality or punctuation. If a child asks a question, then of course this is answered, but the answer is not allowed to distract the class from, or mask, the objective that is being addressed.

Planning a sequence of objectives does not preclude seizing the teachable moment or adapting the objectives at the completion of the first or second session with a book. It is not unusual for teachers to discover after a first or second reading of a text that the objectives chosen for future shared reading sessions are not clearly illustrated, or that the text is not as motivating as first thought. Children do not learn if they are bored and constant revisiting of a text can alienate them. To persevere with a text that has lost its appeal, simply to address a series of meticulously planned objectives, can be counter-productive. It threatens children's enjoyment of the text, their perception of the reading process as satisfying and purposeful, and the worth of shared reading as an effective strategy. In these circumstances, it is common sense to make adaptations to maximise the worth of the future shared reading sessions.

Sequences of objectives always need to be tailored to the needs of the children. Sometimes children clearly grasp a concept or learn to control a strategy much more quickly than one would expect. Conversely, there may be times when the concept or strategy needs to be re-taught in several different contexts before a teacher can confidently move on.

Children are not normally ability-grouped for shared reading sessions because one of the benefits of the teaching strategy is the sharing of a range of interpretations of the text and a variety of reading strategies. Shared reading provides a perfect setting for weaker readers to gain an insight into the ways that effective readers make meaning.

Whole class sessions are common and few classes have the luxury of an extra pair of hands. However, where adult assistance makes grouping possible, it can be based on the needs of the situation. For example, two shared reading sessions run concurrently could involve children in reading two different versions of Cinderella, setting the scene for a re-telling activity later in the Literacy Hour. Alternatively, one shared reading session could involve an information text about frogs, whereas the other could feature a story about frogs. When the class came together, children could talk about the text they had read and could identify the differences between them.

How Do I Select Reading Material?

Traditionally big books have been the source of material for shared reading sessions. The combination of enlarged text and appealing illustrations is attractive to readers. Big books propped on an easel allow teachers to guide the interaction and point to significant parts of the text. However, many innovative teachers have also enlarged poems, chants, songs and class recounts onto flip-charts and some have used overhead transparencies successfully.

If a big book is used, having the text in smaller, individual books increases the chance of children re-reading the text between and beyond the shared reading sessions. It also allows the text to be used for small group sessions using a strategy like guided reading.

One factor that drives the choice of a suitable text is that the text provides a good medium for teaching a chosen objective. For instance, if the objective were to teach the *ea* vowel phoneme, then *Each, Peach, Pear, Plum* by Janet and Allan Ahlberg (Kestrel Books, 1978) would clearly be an excellent choice. It may be that the teacher needs an additional text to reinforce children's learning in guided reading or in an additional shared reading session, and can not find another suitable book. In this case a text could be constructed to meet the need. For example:

> I like meat and I like bread
> I like apples, green and red,
> And sweets and ice-cream for a treat –
> We all like scrummy things to eat!

The choice of reading material can be influenced by a focus on a certain theme, a curriculum area, an author, a text form, and, most importantly, the children's interests. It is crucial that children are introduced to a range of text forms so that they learn how anticipation and awareness of text features and language can enhance comprehension. For example, an effective reader knows that a contents page and an index will be helpful in a search for specific information in a non-fiction book.

It is not essential that an entire text is used in a session. Where time restricts the reading of an entire text, the shared reading should be concluded at an appropriate break. In the case of anthologies and non-fiction material, teachers may demonstrate that the text can be used selectively by reading chosen chapters or selected works. Where fiction material is being used, suitable breaks can be chosen according to events in the story.

What to look for when selecting texts

Fiction	Non-fiction
• Interesting, enjoyable plot • A story-line that children can relate to • Clear, large print, with sentences that are not always confined to one line of print. Some print devices that support meaning are useful, e.g. The bean got **bigger and bigger** • Attractive, relevant illustrations that support and enhance the text • Predictable text, including rhyme, rhythm and repetition • Varied themes • A range of authors and illustrators • Portrayal of different types of characters and settings • Reflection of a variety of cultural contexts	• A recognisable format that is appropriate to the form of writing • Standard conventions such as headings, sub-headings and a contents page. An index is also a desirable feature • Photographs, illustrations and simple diagrams, tables, graphs that support the text • Appropriate language features, e.g. the use of verbs to introduce each step in a procedure • Accurate information

Do I Need to Know the Text Well?

Prereading of the text by the teacher is essential. The teacher needs to be sure that the text is especially well suited for the teaching of the chosen objective. Not only does prereading provide an opportunity for identifying particular text characteristics like graphophonic and grammatical features, rhyme or overall structure, but it also enables the teacher to identify words that might pose problems and to ensure that the level of difficulty is appropriate. Sections of the text may lend themselves to choral reading, whereas the teacher might feel that other parts would provide opportunities for group or individual reading.

Shared reading demands the full attention of teacher and pupils. Pupils need to be comfortably seated where they can see the text clearly, or the point of the session is lost. Motivating, attractive texts, authentic reading purposes and lively, relevant discussion encourage the engagement of a shared reading group. The explicit nature of the teaching in a shared reading session demands that children be focused upon both text and teacher.

Encouraging a safe, supportive atmosphere for shared reading is critical to its success as a teaching strategy. Children who have limited experience with the English language or who lack confidence in their reading ability may initially choose not to join in with the choral reading conducted during the session. These pupils are normally engaged with the text on a personal level and should not be singled out, but rather encouraged and supported until they feel confident enough to join in.

Some children may need guidance about how to accept and build on the suggestions of their peers. It is crucial that all contributions are received positively. Teachers need to model responses that are accepting and interested. Sometimes, if a child's contribution is not what is wanted, it is tempting to say, *'Thank you Daniel. Now, Shari, what do you think?'* This leaves Daniel with the knowledge that his response was somehow lacking and that the teacher knows that Shari will say the right thing! All interactions need to be valued and taken seriously so that every child knows that his or her contribution will be worth offering and that it will receive due consideration. The teacher's responses provide a model for all the children and set the scene for a productive, lively session where all contributions are valued.

Teachers can model how a text can be interpreted in a number of ways and how an opinion about the text can be supported by what the reader already knows and what the text or the pictures tell readers. For example, when reading *Handa's Surprise,* Rashed might comment that seven big bits of fruit would be far too much for one girl to eat, whereupon the teacher could respond, *'I'd never thought of that, but you're quite right. I wonder what Akeyo will do with it?'* Rashed might then suggest that Akeyo could share it with her family or with all her friends, just like he shares things at home. A child might say that Handa was silly not to notice that her basket was getting lighter and lighter and another might suggest that the animals were taking the fruit very gently so that she couldn't feel it. A thorough knowledge of the text can help teachers interpret it effectively and help children make connections between their own experiences and those of the characters in a story or the facts in an information text.

What Resources Will I Need?

Apart from a text that is appropriate, interesting and engaging, an easel is sometimes very useful, as it frees the teacher from reading upside-down in order to enable the children to see the book. Young children, however, usually prefer to gather closely round an adult who is holding the book, at any rate for the first reading, to retain the informal and 'cosy' nature of the session. The easel may come into its own on subsequent readings of portions of text and when children are finding words, or pointing to pictures.

A pointer can also be very useful, when a teacher wants to draw attention to a specific component of the text without covering up the surrounding text with an arm. Children love using a pointer!

Small sticky labels that can be used to cover up words and then removed without damaging the book are extremely useful. Teachers can use them for cloze activities or to draw attention to specific aspects of the text.

A sheet of clear plastic can be clipped to a page of a big book so that words or letters can be underlined or circled using a water-based pen.

A stock of blank 'word cards' is invaluable. Children often need to search through a text, to find:

- a specific letter pattern
- words of a particular class
- sight words
- words that are of special interest to them.

These words can be written on the cards, categorised appropriately and then used for Word Sorts or for displaying in a class Word Bank.

Sometimes props, such as hand puppets, can be used to enhance the reading of a text, but care has to be taken that these do not interfere with the children's focus on the print.

What is the Role of the Teacher?

During a shared reading session the teacher is involved in:

- engaging the children
- reading the text aloud with expression
- directing children to a significant feature of the text
- co-ordinating choral reading
- clarifying, summarising, questioning and extending pupils' contributions
- encouraging discussion about key elements of the text and maintaining the focus on the session objective(s).

How Does Shared Reading Work?

The first reading of any text is dedicated to enjoyment and understanding of the overall meaning. It is relatively uninterrupted, although the teacher may pause to make a comment, such as, *'This bit's really scary, isn't it?'* or *'Oh dear, this is very sad...'*. Subsequent readings of the text allow for different aspects or features to be explored during each session. An objective is seldom totally achieved in one session and frequently needs to be revisited or consolidated on other occasions, usually using a different text. Children can become very bored and alienated if a text is over-used. They love to share in the reading of an old favourite, but become restless if a text is 'flogged to death', however well loved it may be.

Within each text form, the author follows particular conventions. Effective readers learn to anticipate the use of conventions and the more familiar a reader is with these conventions, the easier the text is to read. As readers become more experienced with each form, they are more easily able to anticipate what is to be found in a text, comprehend it and write using the conventions of the form. For this reason, the following outlines include activities divided into those that are suitable for non-fiction texts and those suitable for narrative texts.

One way in which a series of sessions might unfold is suggested for each of these broad text categories. In planning a sequence of sessions, teachers should be guided by the major objectives to be taught, and the features of the text. Other activities planned for the Literacy Hour will be based on the chosen objectives. Major objectives can be selected from the Text, Sentence and Word Levels of the National Literacy Strategy Programme of Teaching Objectives. Some texts will be found to be more versatile than others. Teachers find that, with experience, they develop an 'analytical eye' for text features that tie in with major objectives.

Consideration also needs to be given to the subsequent whole class and small group components of the Literacy Hour. Common sense dictates that if the major objective of the shared reading session is to teach a range of strategies to decode unknown words, then the activities that follow should provide opportunities for pupils to apply those strategies. Guided reading sessions and independent cloze activities are examples of the types of activities that would be suitable. Many other activities are suggested in the *First Steps* books *Word and Sentence Work, Fiction and Poetry* and *Information Texts at Key Stage 1*.

If the focus of the shared reading session was the examination of the features of a particular text form with the intention of having pupils write using that text form, the subsequent activities would reflect a writing emphasis. A balance needs to be maintained between reading and writing in the Literacy Hour.

The activities suggested in the following pages are intended to be a 'dip-in' selection from which teachers can choose, according to the needs of the pupils and the type of text being used. They are not intended to be used as a list to be worked through. All suggested activities will benefit from teacher-adaptation and refinement, especially those that are directed towards a specific text.

Using Non-Fiction Material in a Series of Shared Reading Sessions

Before Reading

Readers need to have a clear understanding of *why* they are reading, *what* they are expected to gain from the reading and *how* they are going to use the information. Before the lesson begins, pupils need to see and hear from the teacher what the focus of the lesson will be. If readers are interested, then their comprehension will be much greater than if they are reading to please their teacher. Young children need to know how to approach a text and how to get the most out of it. Before starting to read teachers need to go through the following procedure.

- **Whetting the appetite and clarifying the purpose.** The teacher's introduction to the text is very important. If, for instance, the chosen book is *This Week,* by Monica Hughes and Susanna Price (Ginn, 1995), a teacher in Reception might say: *'I've found a book I really like about what some children in London do each day of the week. I thought it would be fun to see if they do the same sorts of things that we do. Perhaps when we've read it we could write our own book about what we do and send it to them.'*

- **Activating background knowledge and linking it to what might be in the book.** *'Let's make a chart and write down some of the things that we do so that we can find out if they do the same things as us. Let's see. What do we do on Mondays?'*

MONDAY	TUESDAY	WEDNESDAY	THURSDAY	FRIDAY	SATURDAY	SUNDAY
Bring books back to school. Have Readers' Circle	Do science. Library	Go for a nature walk	Our turn on the roof playground to take home	Go to Assembly. Choose book	Go shopping with Mum	Play football

- **Review and clarify vocabulary.** *'Now we've made our chart, we can be sure that we can read and write all the days of the week. I think the most difficult to read is Saturday. What do you think? What a good thing we know the days of the week.'*

- **Look at text organisation.** *'We used the days of the week to write what we do on our chart. I wonder if the author has used the days of the week to tell us what the London children do? Shall we have a look and see?'*

- **Think about the reading strategy.** *'When we read the book, we're going to look especially hard at the beginning of each word to help us know what it is. Remember, Monday starts with M...mmmm. Each day of the week ends with* **day**, *so that will help too – remember Mon**day**, Tues**day**...'*

Brainstorming and Classifying

When teachers draw attention to the background information that is drawn upon when reading, children begin to understand its importance to comprehension. It promotes active reading as pupils set out to find information that is important to them. Although brainstorming is commonly used to introduce non-fiction texts, it is also a useful process for activating background knowledge before reading fictional material, especially when the text is based on fact or set in a familiar context.

Before children begin to read a piece of text, for example Year 1 or 2 pupils about to read a report on frogs, ask, *'What do you already know about frogs?'* Each suggestion can be written on a card and then the cards can be classified. These categories often form a framework for thinking about the topic. For instance, children might say, *'They can swim. They eat flies. They've got long tongues that pop out. They come from frogspawn and tadpoles.'* These facts, with any others that are forthcoming, can be placed in categories labelled *Where frogs live* (habitat), *What frogs look like* (physical appearance), *What frogs eat* (food), and *How frogs reproduce*.

At this point it is a good idea to ask children if they can think of anything they don't know that they would like to find out about frogs. They might say, *'How does the frogspawn turns into tadpoles? Do they make nests?'* or *'Where do they go to sleep at night?'* These questions are listed and help to provide an additional purpose for reading the book.

Creating frameworks also serves the purpose of introducing pupils to much of the vocabulary they will encounter in the text. Discussion about concepts can include a focus on pronunciation and characteristics of words.

'Before and After' Charts

This prereading strategy is suitable for individuals or groups of children preparing to read information texts. By familiarising children with it in shared reading sessions, they are better prepared to use it when they undertake reading that is not supported by the teacher. The strategy reminds children of what they already know and helps them link this to new information. It also clarifies the purpose for reading.

Before reading, pupils list all they know about a topic to be studied. After reading, they write down what they have learned. They compare the two lists and write down questions that they still need to answer.

Frogs

Before reading	Things we want to know	After reading	Things we still need to find out
They are good swimmers	Where do they live? Do they have nests?		
They eat flies	Do they eat anything else? What do tadpoles eat?		
Frogspawn turns into tadpoles	How do they get the frogspawn? How does it turn into tadpoles?		
Tadpoles turn into frogs	How do tadpoles turn into frogs?		
They are greeny-grey and have long tongues	Are they hot-blooded or cold-blooded?		

Prediction

It is vital that all pupils are involved in prediction because efficient readers are constantly making and revising predictions as they seek to make sense of the text. Invite children to predict from the:

- title
- cover
- table of contents
- pictures, photographs, diagrams

about the following things:

- information they might find in the text
- the sorts of words they are likely to find
- the text structure, e.g. information set out in categories, use of headings.

Prediction activities should be short and stimulating.

Setting a Purpose

Discuss the material and establish why the text is being read, so that pupils can approach the text purposefully. They will then be able to decide whether their purpose has been accomplished when they finish reading.

Encourage them to discuss why they are reading the text. They may offer only one reason, or a whole range of reasons, for example:

- because they are interested in it
- so that they can tell other people what they have found out
- so that they can compare one topic with another
- to find out facts
- because they want to write about it.

Encourage pupils to think about the ways in which they can read a text, so that they begin to understand that a skilled reader uses a whole range of reading strategies, for instance:

- skimming to get an overall picture
- scanning to find a specific bit of information
- reading slowly so that facts can be learned and remembered
- jotting down words or phrases to assist with an oral or written report later on.

Shared reading is an ideal context for demonstrating strategies for different types of reading. Even if pupils are not yet mature enough to use these strategies for themselves, they will remember and use them when they need them later on. Where necessary, jointly constructed charts can be displayed to remind readers of strategies and procedures that have been used.

Ways we can use books	
If we want to see what the book is about	• we can look at the title • we can skim through the book and look at the pictures and diagrams • we can look at the contents page • we can look at the headings
If we want to find a particular fact	• we can look at the contents page and find where it might be • we can scan the section where we think it might be to find a key word • we could look in an index, if there is one
If we want to find a key word quickly	• we look for the first two or three letters

Prereading discussion should be brief and highly focused, or children who are eager to start reading will become bored and lose their motivation. The following discussion guide may be of use.

Discussion Guide

Focus/Objective	Sample dialogue
To engage the children	Teacher: *We were so grateful that Prodeepta brought some tadpoles for us to keep in the classroom, so I hunted in the library and found a book that would tell us all the things we wanted to know about them.* Pupil: *Does it tell us how tadpoles turn into frogs?* Teacher: *We'll have to start reading and see.*
To read non-fiction books and understand that the reader doesn't need to go from start to finish but selects according to what is needed (NLS Year 1, Term 3, Text Level 18)	Teacher: *If we want to find out how tadpoles turn into frogs, will we need to read the whole book?* Pupil: *Yes.* Teacher: *Well, that would certainly be one way of finding out, but can anyone think of a quicker way?* Pupil: *Find a picture of tadpoles turning into frogs and read underneath it.*

Focus/Objective	Sample dialogue
	Teacher: *Let's try and do that first, then we'll see if we could find another way as well.* Pupil: *I want to read the whole book* Teacher: *We'll certainly read the whole book in the end, but let's read the bit about tadpoles first.*
To use awareness of the grammar of a sentence to decipher new or unfamiliar words, e.g. predict text from the grammar, read on, leave a gap and re-read (NLS Year 1 Term 3, Sentence Level 2)	Teacher: *If we come to a word we don't know, what can we do?* Pupil 1: *Sound it out.* Pupil 2: *Look at the picture to see if it helps.* Teacher: *Well done. Yes, we can do both those things. It still may be hard for us, though, as there may be quite a lot of new words that we haven't heard before. If we still can't read a word, what else could we do?* Pupil 3: *Guess.* Teacher: *Yes, we can. We can read to the end of the sentence and think about what would make sense and then read the sentence again and put the word we have guessed into it. Then later on we can look it up in the dictionary to see if we were right.*
To identify simple questions and use the text to find answers. To locate parts of text that give particular information including labelled diagrams and charts (NLS Year 1, Term 3, Text Level 19)	Teacher: *When Prodeepta brought the tadpoles to school yesterday, we thought of lots of things we wanted to know about them. Look, here's our list of questions. Where shall we start?* Pupil 1: *I want to know about where the tadpoles came from? I mean, how did they get there?* Pupil 2: *I want to know whether frogs have nests.* Teacher: *We can find the answers to both those questions. Let's start by looking at the Contents page... Now we can go to the right section and have a look at the pictures first... Look, here's a wonderful diagram of a tadpole turning into a frog. Let's read about it.*

Focus/Objective	Sample dialogue
To use an index and discuss how it is used (NLS Year 2, Term 2, Text Level 18)	Teacher: *We want to find out how tadpoles turn into frogs. One way to do that quickly would be to look in the index. I need to think of a word that I can look for in the index. Can anyone think of one?* Pupil 1: *How tadpoles turn into frogs.* Teacher: *That's certainly what we need to know, but to use the index I need one word. Any ideas?* Pupil 2: *Tadpoles.* Teacher: *Well done. Now, what can I do?* (Silence.) Teacher: *Look, here's the index. It's a long list of words and they're arranged according to the letter of the alphabet they start with. Here's Appearance at the very beginning of the list, because it starts with A. Where will I find Tadpole?* Pupil 3: *Find T.* Teacher: *You're absolutely right. Will you come and help me?*
To build individual collections of new words from reading linked to particular topics (NLS Year 2, Term 2, Word Level 10)	Teacher: *When Rajid and I were looking down the index to find Tadpole we noticed some words that sounded very interesting. If you come across any words you find interesting, don't forget to jot them down later on and put them in your Interesting Words list.*
To evaluate the usefulness of a text for its purpose (NLS Year 2, Term 3, Text Level 18)	Teacher: *We've thought about the questions we want answered, and we've looked in this book to see if we could find the answers by looking at the contents page, the index and at some photographs and diagrams. Do you think this would be a good book for us to read?* Pupil: *It seems to have lots of the answers, but the print is very big and it looks a bit babyish.* Teacher: *It does, doesn't it? Perhaps we should look at this other one that I've got to see if it is any better...*

Note that some comments can focus on several aspects of the shared reading. For example, the comment *'We were so grateful that Prodeepta brought some tadpoles for us to keep in the classroom, so I hunted in the library and found a book that would tell us all the things we wanted to know about them'* makes it clear to the children why the book is being read and motivates them to engage with the text.

It is important that any predictions made about the text are confirmed or rejected at appropriate points in the reading. If time and space permit, making lists of predictions about the text and anticipated vocabulary and displaying them within reach will make it easier to confirm and reject predictions.

During Reading

For the first reading, the teacher and children read primarily for enjoyment and interest. The teacher and children may read in unison, but sometimes the teacher takes over the reading if the text is difficult or the vocabulary unfamiliar. The teacher guides the reading by pointing to the text as it is read. Discussion is driven by the pupils' focus on the meaning of the text. At appropriate breaks in the text, predictions can be confirmed or rejected, information summarised and questions posed about the text to follow. This pattern of reading aloud, pausing to discuss what has been read and what is about to be read, then reading more, is the essence of the shared reading session.

Discussion Guide

Focus/Objective	Sample dialogue
To identify simple questions and use the text to find answers. To locate parts of text that give particular information including labelled diagrams and charts (NLS Year 1, Term 3, Text Level 19)	Teacher: *I think this section has told us the answer to our question about where frogs live – mostly they live in water, but some live on land and some in burrows. Look, the picture is helpful too.*
Confirming or rejecting predictions	Teacher: *We got a lot of things right, didn't we – it says here that frogs have long hind legs to help them leap and swim. We were right, too, when we said they were browny-green, but it also says that there are some frogs that are black and orange, yellow and white or red and green.*
To build individual collections of new words from reading linked to particular topics (NLS Year 2, Term 2, Word Level 10) or To use awareness of the grammar of a sentence to decipher new or unfamiliar words, e.g. predict text from the grammar, read on, leave a gap and re-read (NLS Year 1, Term 3, Sentence Level 2)	Pupil 1: *I like that word 'amph – amphibious'. I'm going to put it in my Interesting Words list.* Pupil 2: *It's a good thing it told us what it meant – living on land and in water – or we'd never have been able to guess.* Teacher: *You were very clever to spot the meaning of the word when you read on, we could never have got it by looking at the picture or sounding out!*

After Reading

A brief reflection on the usefulness of the text concludes the session. Links can be made to the next teaching session or to activities that might follow. It is helpful to revisit the prereading activities to reflect on whether predictions were confirmed or rejected and whether or not questions were answered.

Reviewing the Purpose of Reading
It is essential that the group returns to the objective of the session to decide whether or not it has been achieved.

Review of Brainstorming and Classifying Activity
After reading, pupils need to add to, delete or rearrange the topic framework brainstormed before reading commenced. This is an opportunity to demonstrate how readers link existing knowledge (the framework) to new information (information from the text). Predictions about expected vocabulary can be evaluated in the light of the reading and new words added to the Interesting Words chart.

'Before and After' charts
Revisiting the 'Before and After' chart encourages pupils to think about whether the reading validated their specific background knowledge. Key pieces of information may be confirmed or adjusted to mirror the findings of the first reading.

Second Reading

Before Reading
Pupils summarise the text, helping each other to remember and list the main points. Understandings and skills taught during the first reading are briefly revised.

If it was not possible, because of time constraints, to conduct 'after reading' activities following the first reading, these can be used to review the content of the text and re-activate background knowledge for a second reading.

During Reading
Now that the text content and vocabulary is familiar to the children, it is possible to focus on a single objective, determined by the needs of the group and the curriculum. During reading, the strategy or skill should be modelled so that pupils have a clear understanding of what is being taught and of how and why the skill or strategy is used. Readers need to:

- be aware of and able to use specific strategies for identifying unknown words, using knowledge of phonics, word components, grammar and sense;

- gradually accumulate a bank of common and subject-specific words they can recognise on sight;

- be able to use specific strategies to identify and substantiate important information, for example the main idea;

- be aware of the different levels of comprehension so that they can understand how to comprehend, for example going beyond a literal statement to draw an inference;

- be able to monitor and evaluate their own comprehension so that they can recognise the point at which they cease to understand;
- be aware of organisational patterns of text;
- be able to adopt an objective and know the degree to which it has been achieved.

The Discussion Guide below gives an example of an objective for Reception, Year 1 and Year 2, at the Text, Sentence and Word Levels.

Discussion Guide

Objective	Sharing the Objective (Before Reading)	Reflection/Evaluation of Objective (After Reading)
To expect written text to make sense and to check for sense if it does not (NLS, Reception Year, Sentence Level, 1)	Teacher: *As we read each page of this book, I want you to 'listen to what you are reading' in your head, to make sure it makes sense.* (Each page of the book contains one simple sentence.)	Teacher: *I'm very, very pleased with the way you read each sentence through to yourself to make sure it made sense. Do you remember how at first you read 'On Monday we* brown *our books to school', then you read it through and changed it to 'On Monday we* bring *our books to school'? That shows you are thinking about what you are reading and checking to make sure it makes sense.*
To recognise that non-fiction books on similar themes can give different information and present similar information in different ways (NLS Year 1, Term 3, Text Level 17)	Teacher: *Do you think that if two books are written about the same thing, there is any need to read both of them?* (No response.) Teacher: *Yesterday we read the second book on frogs that I had found. We chose it because the first one looked a bit babyish. Today we'll read the first one. I'd like you to take no notice of the size of the print and the rather babyish look of the book, but think very carefully about what information it is giving us. I'd like you to compare it with the other book and think about what is the same and what is different about it.*	Teacher: *Let's go back to the question we asked ourselves at the beginning of the lesson. Was it helpful to read two books about the same thing, or would one have been enough?* Pupil 1: *I still liked the first one best. It told us about frogs all over the world, not just in Britain. I liked the maps that showed where the different sorts of frogs live.* Pupil 2: *I liked that too, but I thought the second book actually told us more about how to keep tadpoles and what is going to happen to them as they turn into frogs. I mean, the other book just said that they did. I liked all the photographs of tadpoles as they were turning into frogs.* Teacher: *So both books were useful. One told us a lot of facts about frogs across the world and the other lots of tiny details that we wanted to know. We learned a lot from both of them. Now we know it can be very important to read two different books on the same subject.*
To identify and classify words with the same sounds but different spellings (NLS, Year 2, Term 1, Word Level 4)	Teacher: *As we read today, we're going to look out for words that have a different letter pattern, but sound the same. Can anyone remember two words we found yesterday like that?* Pupil: *'Her' and 'learn'.*	Teacher: *Who spotted some words with different letter patterns that sounded the same?* Pupil: *I found 'leap' and 'seed'. Can we put them on the chart?*

Word Identification Strategies

A major focus is placed upon children in Key Stage 1 learning phonics. This emphasis is crucial, as it forms the foundation for a great deal of early reading and writing. Many objectives of shared reading sessions need to be related to the learning and application of phonic understandings.

It is extremely important, however, that a range of word identification strategies is modelled and taught by the teacher, so that pupils do not become so dependent on phonic strategies that they are unable to diversify. Very often a phonic strategy does not work and a pupil needs to be able to know what else can be done to identify an unknown word. Alternative strategies can be modelled both incidentally – when the session has another focus – and explicitly as the major objective of a shared reading session. As a result of the explicit teaching of word identification strategies, pupils will be able to contribute to a growing reference chart, which is refined and extended as further teaching takes place. An example of such a chart is given in Appendix 2 on page 132.

> **What Can I Do if I Don't Know a Word?**
>
> Sound the word out.
>
> Ask myself, 'Is there another way that letter-pattern can sound?'
>
> Re-read the sentence to see if it gives me a clue to the meaning and guess the word.
>
> Check the first letters of the word to see if my guess is right.
>
> Read around the sentence to see if the word is explained in the text.
>
> Ask someone if I am really stuck.

Asking the Teacher

Children should be encouraged to ask questions if something is puzzling them. It is important that the teacher organises enough natural breaks in the reading of the text to provide question opportunities. All questions need to be taken seriously and treated with great respect (*'Jason, I'm so glad you asked that question; it shows that you are thinking very hard'* or *'Mehru, what a good thing you asked, because I'm sure that lots of other people are worried about the same thing'*) so that concerns can be brought to the surface and dealt with on the spot. Young children cannot cope with a time-lag, and waiting until the end of a session can destroy a learning opportunity.

Teachers' Questions

It can be a temptation to ask young children literal questions only. It is very important that inferential and evaluative questions are also asked, so that children are always being encouraged and challenged to think on different levels.

The following examples of literal, inferential and evaluative questions are based on a reading of *This Week,* by Monica Hughes and Susanna Price (Ginn, 1995).

- Literal – What do the children do on Thursday?
- Inferential – Why do you think some children have got their hands up?
- Evaluative – Do you think it's a good idea to have school assemblies?

Finding the Main Idea
During shared reading, pupils may be asked to find the main idea of a paragraph or section of text. The main idea may be stated at the beginning, and it is a good idea to encourage pupils to check this. Sometimes the main idea is implied and readers need to connect information and make inferences. In *This Week*, for instance, there is no text except the days of the week, but the inference is clearly that the children have a routine that they commonly follow. Sometimes a text has no main idea, simply a listing of detail or facts, as might a report on frogs. Efficient readers need to be able to sift the important from the trivial and recognise the main argument or trend of a text, if there is one. The following activities might provide possible starting points:

- creating and changing headings for prereading brainstormed categories;
- writing a jointly composed statement that summarises a section of a text;
- changing sub-headings into questions that reflect the content of the text that follows, to help direct readers to the main idea of the section;
- using a visual model to explain how a main idea relates to the details that support it, for example:

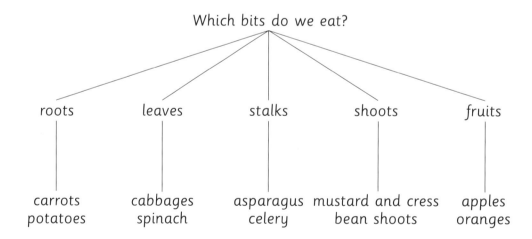

(from *Eating Plants* by Rhonda Jenkins, Ginn 1994)

After Reading

The objective of the shared reading session provides the focus for the remainder of the Literacy Hour. For example, *'In our shared reading session we have been looking for words which, although they have the same letter pattern, sound quite different. Now the group that is going to do guided reading with me will look out for some similar words, using a different book, and the other groups will do Word Sorts, sorting words with the same letter pattern into the way they sound.'*

A range of activities can be conducted with the whole class before children divide for group work. Such activities could include:

- cloze
- sentence transformation
- constructing a flow chart, pyramid or semantic grid together.

A description of these and many other activities can be found in the *First Steps* book *Information Texts at Key Stage 1*.

Subsequent Readings

Teachers need to be able to judge whether or not subsequent readings are a good idea. If children show any signs at all of becoming bored or satiated with a text, it is a good idea to move to another one. It is often wise to continue to address the same objective using different texts to ensure that generalisation takes place.

Subsequent readings will also focus on the same objective if it has not been effectively learned, or may extend the objective further should this be needed. For instance, teaching that a range of texts can offer different insights or ways of presenting the same topic, demands that pupils are exposed to an appropriate range of texts so that each can be evaluated and assessed for its relative worth.

> *Using Fiction and Poetry in a Series of Shared Reading Sessions*

Before Reading

Fiction texts are usually intended to entertain readers. To do this they engender emotions such as excitement, suspense, amusement and sadness. Prereading discussion can focus on the type of fiction or poetry that the reader can expect. For example, *'Do you think this book is going to be about an everyday family, or is it going to be a fantasy?'* or *'I wonder if this poem has been written to make us laugh or to help us to think about how beautiful the world is?'*. Once children have offered their opinions and given their reasons for their judgements, the features of this sort of fiction or poetry could be discussed.

Activating background knowledge is just as important as it is in the prereading discussion of a non-fiction text, but it is designed to help readers think about the structure of fiction and poetry.

Pupils need support as they:

- talk about the difference between reality and fantasy;
- draw on their own life experiences as an aid to understanding;
- discuss new words that they might encounter in the reading;
- predict likely happenings;
- think about the goal of their reading and the objective that has been set for the session.

In the first few minutes of a shared reading session, specific teaching strategies can be used to make sure that the time is productive. Some of these strategies are similar to those already described for non-fiction.

Anticipation
Children learn to anticipate the content or tenor of a poem or story by scanning the text and linking what they see with what they already know about books. Anticipation activities help pupils to understand that readers constantly make connections between what they are reading and their own experience and knowledge. Their experience and knowledge is drawn from life, from television and video and from other books that they have listened to or read.

Pupils can anticipate things about:

- plot
- characters
- setting
- how a story or poem is structured.

Anticipation activities should be brief and lively and should encourage children to become active readers.

Testing the Title
Pupils read and talk about the title, discussing whether or not it invites them to read on. Some titles can tell readers a great deal, some give little away. This in itself can be a topic for talk.

Probing the Pictures
The cover picture can tell potential readers a great deal. It may give clues to the setting, characters and even the plot. Further perusal of pictures can tell readers a great deal about what is coming. It can be especially important to focus on things such as the expressions on the faces of the characters, their attitudes and stances.

Split Images
At the end of Year 1 or in Year 2, children enjoy and gain a great deal from this activity. Two groups sit back to back so that only one group can see the text. The teacher shows one group the illustrations on the first two pages. The group describes what they can see in the illustrations and what they think is happening. The second group is then shown the next two pages and the procedure is repeated, linking their thoughts to the information they have been given by the first group. Turn-taking continues until the book is finished. This activity not only helps children anticipate the story, but also helps them to focus on important features and gloss over peripheral detail.

Brainstorming
Before reading a story, pupils brainstorm anything they think they might know about it. This will vary greatly; for instance, if they are going to read a fairy story or a well-known poem, many children may already have a great deal of knowledge about it. It can sometimes be an excellent idea to choose a folk tale that comes from the homeland of some of the pupils, as this will enable them to share special information about their cultural heritage with their peers.

Discussion Guide

Focus/Objective	Sample dialogue
Motivation	Teacher: *I found this amazing anthology of poetry that really took my fancy, It's called* Dragons, Dinosaurs and Monsters *and the selection of poems was collected by John Foster and Korky Paul*.*
Text form NLS, Year 1, Term 3, Text Level 9: To read a variety of poems on similar themes; and Text Level 11: To collect class and individual favourite poems for class anthologies, participate in reading aloud. Year 2, Term 3, Text Level 6: To read, respond imaginatively and collect examples of humorous poems.	Teacher: *What do you think an anthology is?* Pupil: *I don't know.* Teacher: *I gave you a clue when I told you it was put together, not written, by John Foster and Korky Paul.* Pupil: *Someone else must have written it.* Teacher: *You're nearly there! Remember, I said that the poems were* **collected** *– what does that tell you?* Pupil: *Were they written by lots of people?* Teacher: *Brilliant! Yes, they were. People who collect poems for anthologies usually choose the ones they like best themselves. That's what I'd do, anyway! This anthology is divided into three parts; the first is about dragons, the second dinosaurs and the third monsters. We'll have to decide which section we want to read first, or perhaps we could start by choosing one poem from one section to begin with.*
Cover NLS Year 1, Term 3, Text Level 7: To use titles, cover pages, pictures and 'blurbs' to predict the content	Teacher: *Does the cover give us any idea of what sort of poems might be inside the book?* Pupil: *Funny ones. I love the dragons, they look great!*
Author NLS Year 2, Term 2, Text Level 11: To identify and discuss favourite poems and poets, using appropriate terms (poet, poem, verse, rhyme etc)	Teacher: *We've said that the poems were collected by those two people. Now let's look at the list of people who actually wrote them.* Pupil: *Lots and lots of people.* Teacher: *Yes, there must be more than twenty different poets. Have we read anything else by any of them do you suppose. Let me see... yes, here's a name we know – X.J.Kennedy – do you remember we read a very funny book of his called* The Phantom Ice-Cream Man?**
Illustrator NLS Year 1, Term 3, Text Level 7: To use titles, cover pages, pictures and 'blurbs' to predict the content	Teacher: *The illustrations are absolutely fantastic. Let's see who did them. It's funny, but it doesn't seem to say. Oh yes, here it is, in the tiny print under the publisher's information – selection by John Foster and illustrations by Korky Paul. That explains it, they both did different jobs. It's a bit unusual not to say so on the front cover, though.*
Blurb NLS Year 1, Term 3, Text Level 7: To use titles, cover pages, pictures and 'blurbs' to predict the content	Teacher: *Let's read the blurb on the back of the cover to see what the poems are about. Here's three books of poems in one about every kind of dragon, dinosaur and monster you can think of... I can't wait to start, can you?*

* Oxford University Press, 1991
** Curtis Brown, 1979

During Reading

For the first reading, children and teacher read primarily for enjoyment, fun and interest. Very often in Key Stage 1, the teacher reads the text through with a great deal of expression to maximise comprehension and assist children with word identification. After this the teacher guides the reading and the children join in as they feel they can. Sometimes individuals may be allocated different lines to read, and at a later stage they may take parts, as in Readers' Theatre.

Children often find poetry difficult to read on sight and gain confidence if they are given a strong lead at first. If a story or poem has a repetitive refrain, pupils love to join in and may be encouraged to use any actions that are appropriate. The teacher guides the reading by pointing to the text as it is read. Discussion is driven by pupils' focus on the meaning of the text or their delight in an emotive use of words. At appropriate breaks in the text, predictions can be confirmed or rejected, and ideas sought about the text that is to follow. Breaks can also be used to return to the chosen focus of the reading.

Discussion Guide

Focus/Objective	Sample dialogue
Confirming or rejecting predictions	Teacher: *Louise was right – all the dragons have fire coming out of their mouths.*
Reading aloud together NLS Year 2, Term 2, Text Level 10: To comment on and recognise when the reading aloud of a poem makes sense and is effective.	Teacher: *We've got four groups, so each one will read one verse, then we'll all join in for the last verse. This poem, 'The Last Dragon' by Ian Larmont, is rather sad, so I think we'd better read each verse rather more slowly and softly until we almost fade out at the end.*

After Reading

A brief reflection on the poem or story concludes the session. Links can be made to the activities to follow and to the guided reading session that one group will be undertaking. There should be a brief revisiting of any prereading activities that may have taken place.

Second Reading

Before Reading

To re-orient the class to a second reading of a text, it is useful to ask pupils to take part in a brief retell of what they remember of the text. Understandings and skills taught through the first shared reading can be briefly revised.

During Reading

The objective of the second of a series of shared reading sessions usually moves from a broad, general focus, such as a consideration of the text form or a sharing of reader response, to a single, highly focused objective, such as learning to use a specific word identification strategy. This objective will be determined by the needs of the class and the demands of the curriculum. During reading, pupils need to see processes modelled so that they understand how competent readers construct meaning and respond to text.

Readers need to:

- be able to use specific strategies to identify and substantiate important information, for instance, to identify the reasons for events in stories and how these are linked to the overall plot structure;

- be aware of inferential meaning as well as literal meaning and understand how to begin to draw out evaluative meanings;

- be able to monitor their own comprehension and know what to do if they fail to understand;

- use specific word identification strategies to enable them to read unfamiliar words;

- be aware of the organisational patterns of text;

- relate what they are doing and accomplishing back to the objectives of the session.

The Discussion Guide below gives an example of one objective – to notice the difference between spoken and written forms of language – and how this might be discussed in a shared reading session.

Discussion Guide

Focus/Objective	Sample dialogue
Reception, Text Level 4; Year 1, Term 1, Text Level 3; Year 1, Term 2, Text Level 4; Year 1, Term 3, Text Level 3; Year 2, Term 1, Text Level 3; Year 2, Term 3, Text Level 3: To notice the difference between spoken and written forms.	Teacher: *Can anyone find some words in this poem, 'A Stegosaurus is for Life' by Trevor Millum, that paint a wonderful picture for us, but that we'd never use if we were talking to each other?* Pupil 1: *A fern-decked valley.* Teacher: *Excellent. What might we have said if we were just talking?* Pupil 1: *The valley's full of ferns.* Teacher: *Well done. Anybody else?* Pupil 2: *The sun's fierce glare.* Teacher: *And what might we have said?* Pupil 2: *Away from the awful heat of the sun.*

Word Identification Strategies

Pupils need to know many strategies they can call on to help them identify unknown words. In Key Stage 1 they tend to rely very heavily on phonic strategies, and this is quite appropriate and often works well. However, there is no doubt that a purely phonic approach will sometimes fail them. When it does, they need to know exactly what to do, or their reading will abruptly stop. Pupils need to learn to use not only phonics to help them, but also grammar and meaning. Their innate knowledge of grammar will tell them when something doesn't sound right. They will then be able to work out whether the word they want is a noun, verb or adjective, for instance. Although they may not yet be able to name these classes of words, they can clearly identify them by their function in a sentence. They can then use this grammatical knowledge in conjunction with their understanding of the meaning of a sentence to make a good attempt to identify the word they need. They are then able to check on the word they have come up with by looking at the first few letters. The Discussion Guide below provides an example of the dialogue that could surround such teaching and learning.

Discussion Guide

Focus/Objective	Sample dialogue
NLS Year 1, Term 1, Sentence Level 1&2: To expect written text to make sense and to check for sense if it does not. To use awareness of the grammar of a sentence to deciphernew or unfamiliar words, e.g. predict text from the grammar, read on, leave a gap and re-read. (This objective is repeated for each term of each Year Level thereafter.)	Teacher: *Let's read that again.* Pupil 1: *And he began to run* *Chatting the daylight away to the west...* Teacher: *Think about it. I know it's poetic language, but have another think. Would the dragon* chat *the daylight?* Pupils: *No.* Teacher: *How can we find out what it really says?* Pupil 1: *Sound it out. Ch-a-s-ing, chassing.* Teacher: *That's a problem, I don't think we've quite got it yet. What did we say we should do if we couldn't get a word?* Pupil 2: *Read the whole sentence and leave a gap to help us see what it might be;* *And he began to run —— the daylight away to the west...* Pupil 3: *And he began to run* *Catching the daylight away to the west...* Teacher: *That makes much more sense, but let's check it to make sure.* Pupil 3: *There's no h and no t, so it can't be right, but it does make more sense. I know, chasing!* *And he began to run* *Chasing the daylight away to the west...*

The lines of poetry are taken from 'The Dragon' by Daphne Lister in the anthology *Dragons, Dinosaurs and Monsters,* selected by John Foster and illustrated by Korky Paul (Oxford University Press, 1991).

Children's Questions

Children need to be actively encouraged to ask questions when there is a pause in the reading of the text. Young children need to have instant answers, as they are not able to 'hold' their questions until later. They may also need help in framing their questions and being able to move from the specific problem to the generalised solution. This might involve the use of several examples and ongoing opportunities to practise what has been learned.

Teachers' Questions

Teachers need to be very careful to provide a good balance of literal, inferential and evaluative questions. Even young children are able to make sensible inferences, provided that the context of the question is familiar to them and they can draw on their own experience. Evaluative questions are more difficult both to frame and to answer, but if children are not exposed to them, they may not extend their thinking as they should.

The following examples of literal, inferential and evaluative questions are based on a reading of the poem 'The Grateful Dragon' by Raymond Wilson.

- **Literal** – Why was the dragon starving?
- **Inferential** – Why did the King want to kill the dragon?
- **Evaluative** – What do you think we could learn from this story?

After Reading

The objective of the shared reading session is built upon during the remainder of the Literacy Hour. It is very important that all the activity and the guided reading that follows reinforces, consolidates and sometimes extends the learning that has taken place in the shared reading session. Several complementary objectives can be combined.

An example of complementary objectives that can provide the focus for a whole Literacy Hour, starting with shared reading is given overleaf.

Complementary Objectives	Components of Literacy Hour
Word Level Year 2, Term 1, 10: Children should be taught new words from reading, building individual collections of significant words **Sentence Level** Year 2, Term 1, 2: To find examples of words and phrases that link sentences, e.g. after, meanwhile, during, before, then, next, after a while **Text Level** Year 2, Term 1, 1, 4 & 11: To reinforce and apply Word Level skills through shared reading; To understand time and sequential relationships in stories; To use the language of time (see Sentence Level Work) to structure a sequence of events, e.g. 'when I had finished...', 'suddenly...', 'after that...'	**Shared reading (second session)** Re-read the story of Cinderella, picking out and writing on cards all the words and phrases that tell the reader *when* things happen, or that join parts of a sentence together, telling *why*. Some words and phrases found might be: *Once upon a time* *After* *When* *While* *Then* *Later on* *After a while* *At midnight* *After a few days* *and* *...because...* *... as...* *...since...* **Whole class activity** Physical Sentence Manipulation activity: • Child 1 holds up sentence stem: *Cinderella cried.* • Child 2 stands beside Child 1 holding a conjunction, e.g. *when.* • The rest of the class make up a sentence ending, e.g. *her sisters would not let her go to the ball.* • Child 3 holds up the ending to complete the sentence. The procedure is repeated, using the same sentence beginning but a different conjunction. Children see if the first ending still fits. If it does, they leave it; if not, they invent a different ending. **Group Work** Each group is given a sentence beginning and a range of conjunctions. They invent suitable endings. The group of children who may need scaffolded support are given sentence beginnings, conjunctions and suitable endings, which they match up. One group undertakes guided reading with the teacher. They use a different text, but continue to focus on the use of conjunctions. **Reflection Time** Children discuss what they have learned and jointly construct a chart of 'joining words' that will help them in their writing. They add some of the words to their personal word class lists in their Spelling Journals.

Many other activities are described in the *First Steps* book *Fiction and Poetry at Key Stage 1*, for example:

- Retells
- Story mapping
- Transformation
- Innovation
- Story grammar
- Text reconstruction
- Character ratings
- Report cards
- Wanted posters
- Character interviews
- Story sociograms.

Subsequent Readings

Subsequent shared reading sessions can extend the focus of the previous reading or take on a new focus. It is crucial that the teacher gauges pupils' enthusiasm for the text and uses a new text if the current one is being over-used and is becoming stale. In most instances, it is a good idea to pursue or consolidate the achievement of an objective by using more than one text to ensure that generalisation takes place and that the pupils' use of a skill or strategy is not tied to one specific context.

Guided Reading

Guided reading is a term that describes a range of explicit teaching approaches that have common elements. Some of these approaches have been labelled Directed Silent Reading (DSR), Directed Reading and Thinking Activity (DRTA) and Reciprocal Reading (RR). As the title implies, guided reading involves a purposeful and pre-determined focus on reading and thinking. It is a concentrated procedure for engaging pupils with a text, supporting them in their use of reading strategies, and rehearsing the behaviours of independent reading.

A guided reading session involves a small group of pupils seated with the teacher, silently reading the same unfamiliar text. Children in early Key Stage 1 will probably sub-vocalise, but should be praised for 'reading to themselves'. If they read aloud to the teacher, the session loses its impact and simply becomes an opportunity for teachers to listen to children reading, which is not the aim of guided reading. Even young children can quietly read a picture book, or one with very little print, to themselves, if given guidance and support by the teacher. The frequent breaks for focused discussion help to keep the children on track and ensure that concentration is maintained. Teachers may sometimes decide to give a group of children who are experiencing difficulties a book that has been the focus of a shared reading session, in order to enhance their self-esteem as readers.

The reading of the text is preceded by and regularly interspersed with group discussion about what is being read (the content), how it is organised (the text structure), the type of language used (language features) and how it is being read (the reading process). The specific objective chosen for the session will dictate which of these aspects of reading becomes the focus of a session. It is important that the objective of the session is quite clear to the children and that they are able to focus on only one objective for a specific session.

At appropriate breaks, an observer would expect to hear a summary of the text read, a question posed, a range of answers offered, a word clarified or a question raised that demands further reading. Discussion is guided by the teacher but generated by the pupils. Oral reading occurs if pupils are asked to substantiate the answer to a question or validate their predictions about the text.

Although guided reading approaches may vary in their focus, they have many common elements. In guided reading:

- there is a clearly defined purpose to the reading;
- pupils work in groups of up to six for at least 10 minutes at least once a week (two groups may undertake guided reading in any one literacy lesson);
- the teacher guides the reading, although the role of the teacher may vary;
- pupils all read the same book which is assigned by the teacher and is unfamiliar to the children;
- pupils are grouped according to their reading abilities, needs and the purpose of the session;
- most of the reading is done silently – reading aloud is reserved for substantiation.

Guided reading enables pupils to:

- use their reading skills in a supportive setting;
- compare their interpretations of the text with others;
- practise strategies for making meaning at Word, Sentence and Text Levels;
- read silently and think critically in a co-operative environment;
- receive support as they monitor their own reading.

Guided reading enables teachers to:

- explicitly support pupils in their application of comprehension strategies;
- monitor the comprehension of individuals;
- model how effective readers monitor and manage their comprehension;
- explicitly support pupils in their application of word identification strategies;
- monitor which word identification strategies a pupil is using and how effectively they are being used;
- model the use of word identification strategies that are not well understood or applied.

What is the Difference Between Shared and Guided Reading?

The path to proficient reading is rarely linear. Pupils require support and challenge at different times. While shared and guided reading provide for both these needs at given times, shared reading is considered to be the more supportive because the teacher leads the reading of the text. In shared reading, the reading is done aloud – and often in chorus – so the decoding demands on the pupil are limited. Like a passenger on a tandem bicycle, the pupil is following the skilled cyclist (the reader) and listening to his or her 'think-alouds': *'Let's make sure we're balanced before I push off with my foot to get some speed... now I'm peddling hard because the faster I go, the easier it is to balance.'* At times the passenger might pedal (join in with the reading), but the comfort zone for the learner is maintained as the decisions are made and the impetus set by the leader.

On the other hand, if the analogy is extended to guided reading, the cyclist is on his or her own bicycle. The mentor is ever watchful as the learner experiments with what he or she can do, pushing off and practising on a surface that is not too hazardous! This is similar to what happens in guided reading when the teacher asks a directing question and pupils read silently to consider a response.

One of the key differences between the two strategies is the degree of independence expected of the reader. This is shaped by the context of the reading and the ways in which the teacher interacts with the pupils.

Fundamental to a successful shared reading session are the non-threatening environment, the invitation to participate and the open-ended questions that explore the text. This constitutes reading with a large group of children in a most active, interactive and enjoyable way. Teacher modelling is interspersed with the questions and observations of pupils who are thoroughly engaged with both the text and the teacher demonstrations.

Guided reading, however, is a step closer to independence. Pupils are grouped for a specific purpose, matched with a text that will extend their comprehension and word identification skills and involved in repeated rehearsal of the skills required for independent reading. Silent reading and critical thinking provide the basis for in-depth discussions about the text and the reading strategies used to unravel it.

In broad terms, this is the carefully prepared opportunity for the pupil to apply the reading skills and strategies demonstrated by the teacher in a shared reading session. This is 'reading with' the teacher in an intensive, reflective way.

Shared reading	Guided reading
Large, mixed ability groups or whole classes	Small groups of similar ability
Features a big book or an enlarged text	Pupils have copies of the same text
Teacher and pupils read aloud	Reading is mostly silent
Sessions are 10 – 15 minutes long	Sessions are 15 – 20 minutes long
Texts may be familiar and are re-read several times	Text is unfamiliar
Lots of teacher modelling	Lots of teacher questioning and guidance so that the focus is maintained

When Do I Use Guided Reading?

The group work component of the Literacy Hour is tailor-made for guided reading. Pupils will have already participated in the shared reading or writing session at the beginning of the hour and will have been introduced to and been specifically taught about the specific objective(s) that they are going to pursue in their guided reading session. Remaining groups will be actively engaged in related independent activities while the guided reading group is with the teacher.

Beyond the Literacy Hour, opportunities for a more informal use of the guided reading strategy arise in many curriculum areas. In these cases it is possible to work slightly less intensively with a larger group or with the whole class.

How Do I Choose my Session Objectives?

It is most profitable to continue to build on the objectives chosen for the shared reading session, which provide the platform for and the link with all subsequent components of the hour. It has already been explained how it is possible and desirable to choose objectives at the Text, Sentence and Word Levels that complement and support each other, so that pupils view these objectives not as separate entities, but as a cohesive focus for their reading activities (see page 59).

Objectives are clearly shared with all the pupils at the commencement of the hour. Teacher and pupils revisit them at intervals throughout the hour to ensure that a sharp focus is maintained and that pupils are able to monitor their progress towards their achievement. Discussion Guides offering examples of objectives that can be taught in a guided reading session, and showing how these objectives can be addressed on a regular basis by using specific questions, are given on pages 70, 73 and 77. The Discussion Guides can also provide a framework for conducting a guided reading session.

How are Pupils Grouped for Guided Reading?

Pupils are normally grouped for guided reading according to their ability. Interests and needs are also important considerations. The text needs to reflect the reading ability of the group and, if the same text is used, this demands that each member of the group is operating at more or less the same level. If the session is to flow smoothly, all need to read at about the same rate, or the questioning structure will falter. It would be disruptive if faster readers were obliged to wait for slower children to catch up.

This context is very different from shared reading, when a mixed ability group is of benefit to everybody. Weaker children can benefit from the strategies described and demonstrated by more able readers, and able readers can become aware of and consolidate the skills they are using.

How Do I Select Reading Material?

Text can take the form of anything that is currently relevant to the curriculum, for instance, stories, poems, letters or simple recounts and reports. Textless picture books and familiar, well-illustrated stories can be used with great success with children who are Role Play readers.

The selected text should be one that the group can read with approximately 90 per cent accuracy. An ideal choice would allow pupils to be supported by some knowledge of the content, but challenged by some vocabulary and some of the main ideas. Guided reading enables the group to work together, refining and reviewing the input of individuals, so that a text that would be marginally difficult for the group can become accessible through the guidance of teacher questioning and group interaction.

Each pupil needs to have a copy of the text, which should consist of a complete entity – in the sense that the purpose for reading can be accomplished by the end of the session. It is vital that the text is unseen so that prediction and confirmation skills can be used effectively and the teacher can gain invaluable insights into the strategies used by pupils as they strive to identify unknown words. It is important that the text is relevant and interesting.

Do I Need to Know the Text Well?

Prereading of the text by the teacher is essential. The teacher needs to be sure that the text provides sufficient opportunities for pupils to use the strategy or skill they are being taught. Guiding questions need to be formulated in advance and natural breaks identified when pupils can be asked to summarise a paragraph, confirm or reject a prediction or talk about how they were able to identify an unknown word.

It makes sense for teachers to catalogue, store and share their guided reading ideas for particular texts. Over a short period of time, a school could build up a useful bank of guided reading packages to accompany multiple copies of texts. Teachers, and ultimately children, benefit from this simple sharing of expertise and experience.

What Sort of Questions Should I Ask in Guided Reading?

Part of the preparation for guided reading involves devising questions to ask at key places in the text. To prevent teacher questioning from becoming interrogative and inhibiting discussion, the emphasis is on focused questioning that requires reading between and beyond the lines. The examples below clarify the difference between questions at the literal, inferential and evaluative levels.

Answers to literal questions can be read directly from the text. It is simply a matter of locating the answer. For example, the following questions all relate to 'The Pet' by Tony Bradman, in *Dragon Poems* collected by John Foster (Oxford University Press, 1991).

- Answers to **literal questions** can be found in the text. It is simply a matter of locating them. For example:
    - What did Mum say was NOT to be bought with the money?
    - What colour was the pet?

- Answers to **inferential questions** are found between the lines, and can only be decided by searching for clues and inferring their meaning. For example:
    - What sort of a pet was it? How do you know?
    - Do you think it was wise of Mum to say that the money could be spent on anything except sweets?

- Answers to **evaluative questions** lie beyond the text and require readers to draw on their personal knowledge and experience. For example:
    - Would you like to have a pet like that?
    - Why was that pet so specially important?
    - What do you think would happen if you took a pet home without asking first?

Skilled questions maximise the potential of the reading material and generate high-level thinking and discussion. They also provide an excellent model for pupils who need to adopt self-questioning strategies and learn how to read 'into' a text to answer different types of questions. Generally, inferential and evaluative questions are open-ended and therefore the pupils may give a range of answers. It is very useful to ask how pupils reached their conclusions. For example: *'I really knew the pet was a dragon because I looked at the picture, but even if I hadn't I'd have guessed, because of the scales and burning eyes and the wings and gleaming fangs, but most of all because of the breath being orange flame and the ears hissing with steam.'*

Pupils also need to justify their opinions by referring both to the text and to their own life experience. For example: *'My mum would kill me if I brought a pet home without asking, even if it was a kitten or a puppy and not a dragon. There'd be how much it would cost to feed and who'd look after it if we went away and things like that. I think the last verse tells that the mum in the poem wouldn't be too pleased either.'*

Directing questions, key words or sentences and similar prompts can be pencilled on the teacher's copy of the text or attached on temporary adhesive notes.

Reading – Section 2

> **How Do I Manage the Rest of the Class while I am Working with One Group?**

Guided reading is a small group, teacher-directed activity. Pupils not involved in guided reading need to be engaged in familiar, purposeful, independent tasks and have a clear understanding that the teacher is not available for inquiries. Many activities that fulfil all these requirements are described in the other books in this series.

Some useful guidelines are as follows.

- The whole class should be taught a range of activities that are open-ended in that they can accommodate any content that currently needs to be taught and can support objectives at the Word, Sentence and Text Levels. These should be introduced gradually until the class has a wide repertoire of such activities that can be used without having to think consciously about organisation or methodology – all the attention can be directed towards content. Examples of such activities are Word Sorts, Sentence Manipulation, Story Mapping.

- It is often possible to use the whole-class activity time after the conclusion of the shared reading or writing session to model the activity which will follow in small group time.

- Pupils should always know exactly what they are expected to do should they finish their activity ahead of time – one idea could be to prepare as a group for the reflection time at the end of the hour, while another might be to start to read their home reading book or a library book.

- It should be clearly understood that only in the case of a dire emergency, such as someone feeling sick, should the teacher be interrupted. Even small children are able to abide by this rule if they know exactly what they should do while they wait for the teacher to finish. Children should be highly praised for working independently without fuss.

While children in the guided reading group are silently reading sections of text, the teacher may be observing reading behaviours such as pointing, using picture cues, sub-vocalising, how a child reacts if he or she seems to be 'stuck', and speed of reading. This does not preclude a quick, authoritative glance around the room or a brief directing comment to those who are working independently, as long as the flow of the guided reading session is not disrupted.

Pupils involved in guided reading require the oral, social and cognitive skills necessary for effective group discussion. These skills include:

- taking turns
- asking for clarification or help
- being interested in what others have to say and receiving their remarks positively
- offering ideas, comments, feedback
- paraphrasing
- learning to disagree diplomatically.

What Resources Will I Need?

Apart from multiple copies of the text, guided reading simply requires a quiet space for the children to sit, read and interact. Ideally the seating would be arranged to enhance discussion and would allow easy access to supporting reference materials such as wall banks displaying interesting words or words relating to the topic being considered. A board or flip-chart is useful for recording predictions and the brainstormed key words. Some teachers also have success in building children's questioning skills by providing prompt cards, which provide some examples of sentence stems.

I wonder why	I didn't understand
I worked out what that word was by	I found the answer by
I want to find out more about	If I had written this book I would have
I like this part because	I don't like this part because
This bit reminds me of	One word I don't understand is

While it is often a good idea to use some 'props', such as puppets, in a shared reading session, these can be a distraction in guided reading when the children need to be encouraged to focus their entire attention on the text.

What is my Role?

The role of the teacher in a guided reading session varies according to the purpose of the lesson and how familiar the group is with the procedure. However, the role is essentially one of group facilitator. The teacher clarifies the task and the purpose, guides the reading by asking stimulating questions, and links and values the contributions of each child. The teacher does not control the discussion, but facilitates it, ensuring all group members are engaged in making meaning. In doing this, the teacher is also modelling an enjoyment and interest in reading.

Initially the children in the group may be dependent on the teacher for directing questions, but after four or five lessons most children can begin to frame their own questions, even if these are modelled directly on the questions they have heard the teacher use.

Role Play Readers

These children clearly need a great deal of support, but it is important that even they are able to exercise a degree of independence as they gain in confidence and skill. Young children enjoy and are quite capable of 'reading' a book independently, by looking at the pictures and thus following a simple story. This is particularly true in the context of guided reading when the teacher punctuates the session with opportunities for children to share perceptions with the group and receive additional guidance to keep them on track.

Experimental Readers

These children can demonstrate a high degree of independence as they 'creatively' read their text. Once again, the pauses for discussion and guidance are crucial. The focus should be placed on affirming their ability to make meaning from pictures while praising them for their determined attempts to derive meaning from the text. If the need to establish an accurate rendering of word-by-word reading is over-emphasised, the search for meaning will be hindered rather than helped. Children need to be encouraged as they go through a period of 'creative invention' based on the text before they reach the stage of 'word focus' that follows this period. The phase of experimentation in reading, anchored by and based loosely on periodic word identification, affirms the over-riding importance of comprehension.

Early Readers

These children should be able to operate with a high degree of independence. It is important that the teacher's goal is always to move towards independent functioning. Children need to be highly praised for using initiative and imagination and 'having a go'. It can be too easy to create dependency and inadvertently inhibit independence by insisting on correctness and providing too much support.

NOTE: *Although questions from the range of comprehension levels provide opportunities for the teacher to observe the depth of understanding of individuals, this is not the primary purpose. Nor is guided reading a context for extended oral comprehension questioning that resembles interrogation. The primary aim of questioning in a guided reading session is to generate discussion rather than stifle it. The responsibility for answering questions arising from the text rests squarely with the group. The teacher simply provides support in this process by clarifying and re-framing questions where necessary, and focusing on how the questions are answered to ensure that comprehension strategies are encouraged.*

How Does Guided Reading Work?

The following outline is intended to provide a sense of how the interaction between teacher and children might unfold in a guided reading session.

Guided reading strategies are characterised by three definite phases of activity: before, during and after reading. While it is not essential that teachers ask the generic questions shown in the Discussion Guide on page 70, using a flexible but consistent sequence makes the guided reading session predictable and ensures that objectives are addressed on a regular basis.

Reading – Section 2

Only one objective would be the key focus of the session. The remaining objectives receive attention on an incidental basis, and are included simply to show why the teacher guides the reading in the way described. The lesson is not intended to be a blueprint for any one year level. The objectives listed are relevant for all pupils in Key Stage 1, who are Role Play, Experimental or Early readers.

The objectives are drawn from the National Literacy Strategy Programme of Teaching Objectives. Two outlines have been provided, one for a non-fiction text and another for fiction. Although this distinction is simplistic, it illustrates how the guided reading session 'signposts' differ in each instance. When reading an information text, devices such as headings, sub-headings and diagrams allow the reader to negotiate the text. Consequently a guided reading session should be arranged around these markers. In Key Stage 1 it can be difficult to find information texts that are adequate in this respect. Sometimes non-fiction can be disguised as a story, or not well structured, which can be confusing for readers. If this is the case, the teacher's guiding questions are even more important, as they can be designed to clarify the text structure for the reader. Fortunately more and more well-structured information texts are being produced.

When reading narrative, an understanding of elements such as setting, characters and plot will help readers deepen and extend their comprehension of a story. Developing readers need to be shown how effective readers use this awareness of text features to support their comprehension.

Using Non-Fiction in a Guided Reading Session

Objectives have been drawn from several year levels to show how a skill is expected to develop over time. It will be seen that the teacher's questions can be adapted to meet the needs of the different year levels without difficulty.

Before Reading
Discussion Guide

Objective	Sample dialogue
Year 1, Term 1, Text Level 17: To use terms 'fiction' and 'non-fiction', noting some of their differing features, e.g. layout, titles, contents page, use of pictures, labelled diagrams. Year 2, Term 3, Text Level 13; To understand the distinction between fact and fiction; to use terms 'fact', 'fiction' and 'non-fiction' appropriately. Year 1, Term 3, Text Level 18: To read non-fiction books and understand that the reader doesn't need to go from start to finish, but selects according to what is needed.	Teacher: *What sort of a book do you think this will be?* Pupil: *I think it's a non-fiction book.* Teacher: *What makes you think so?* Pupil: *The title says 'Frogs'. So it sounds like non-fiction, and the frog on the cover is a real frog. I mean, it's not dressed up or anything.* Teacher: *If you look inside the book, is there anything else that helps you know that it's a non-fiction book?* Pupil 1: *It's got an index.* Pupil 2: *It's got photos and diagrams.* Pupil 3: *It's got headings and things – and it's got a contents page.* Teacher: *I think you've spotted all the important features of a non-fiction book between you – well done!*

Objective	Sample dialogue
Year 2, Term 3, Text Level 17: To skim-read title, contents page, illustrations, chapter headings and sub-headings, to speculate what a book might be about. Year 1, Term 3, Text Level 21: Understand the purpose of contents pages and indexes and to begin to locate information by page numbers and words by initial letter. Year 2, Term Three, Text Level 16: To scan a text to find specific sections, e.g. key words or phrases, subheadings.	Teacher: *Well, we wanted to find out more about frogs, so I've found a book that will help us. What did we say we particularly wanted to find out?* Pupil 1: *Where they live.* Pupil 2: *How frogspawn turns into tadpoles.* Teacher: *Yes – those were two important things we wanted to know. How can we use this book to help us?* Pupil 3: *Read it.* Teacher: *All of it? Well, I suppose we could, but we really want to know those two things more than anything else. So how can we find the answers to those particular questions?* Pupil 1: *Find the right bit to read.* Teacher: *Well done. Now the word for where animals live is 'habitat'. So what do we do next?* Pupil 1: *Look in the index.* Pupil 2: *Look on the contents page.* Teacher: *You're both right. Let's try it and see...*
Year 2, Term 1, Text Level 14: To note key structural features. Year 2, Term 3, Text Level 15: To use a contents page and index to find way about a text.	Teacher: *We've had a look at the title and contents page. Now, flip through the book. Can you tell me how the text is arranged?* Pupil 1: *I can see headings telling what each bit is about.* Teacher: *Can you find out if the headings match the Contents?* Pupil 1: *Yes, the big heading at the top of the page is the same.* Teacher: *That's important, because it shows that if we use the Contents page properly, we can get straight to the information we need. Now, what else can you see?* Pupil 2: *I can see photos...*
Year 2, Term 2, Text Level 19: To read flow simple flow charts or diagrams that explain a process.	Teacher: *We'll start by finding out how frogspawn turns into frogs. You've found where it says 'Reproduction' in the contents page. Now, when you've found the right page, what can you see?* Pupil: *A circle drawing.* Teacher: *It's called a diagram. Let's look at it...*

Objective	Sample dialogue
Year 2, Term 3, Text Level 14: To pose questions and record these in writing, prior to reading non-fiction to find answers.	Teacher: *In our shared reading session we decided that there were a lot of things we wanted to find out about frogs. Here's the list of things we said. Can someone choose something that we would all like to find out?* Pupil 1: *Frogspawn.* Pupil 2: *Where they live.* Teacher: *Yes those are two very important things. Can anyone turn the words 'frogspawn' into a question that we can find the answer to?* Pupil 1: *What is frogspawn?* Pupil 2: *How does frogspawn turn into frogs?* Teacher: *Those are two very good questions. Perhaps we can combine them – 'What is frogspawn and how does it turn into frogs?'. We'll find out the answer to that question first, then we'll deal with the other one. I'll write our question on this long strip of paper and pin it up here, to remind us why we are going to read this text.*

During Reading

During the guided reading session, pupils are engaged in the silent reading of a section of text. Experimental and Early readers will often sub-vocalise as they read. This is quite appropriate. At pre-determined breaks in the text, the teacher directs the children to reflect on the section completed.

Discussion Guide

Objective	Sample dialogue
Year 1, Term 1, Text Level 1: To reinforce and apply their word-level skills through guided reading; and Text Level 2: to use phonological, contextual, grammatical and graphic knowledge to work out, predict and check the meaning of unfamiliar words and to make sense of what they read. Year 1, Term 2, Text Level 1: To reinforce and apply their Word Level skills. Year 2, Terms 1, 2 & 3, Text Level 1 & 2, Sentence Level 1, at most Year levels: To use awareness of grammar to decipher new or unfamiliar words, e.g. to predict from the text: to read on, leave a gap and re-read. Year 1, Terms 1, 2 & 3, Sentence Level 1: To expect reading to make sense and check if it does not.	Teacher: *Did any of the words give you any trouble?* Pupil 1: *I found this one hard – speckled.* Teacher: *How did you work out what it said?* Pupil 1: *Well, I read the whole bit again to see what would make sense. It says 'The frog's back may be grey, yellow, brown or speckled.' I looked at the picture and it had sort of spots, so I thought it must be spotted, but when I looked, it didn't say that. Anyway, I looked at the first half of the word and got 'speck' and after that it was easy! Then I read it again and it made sense.* Teacher: *Is everyone quite comfortable with what they've read?* Pupil 2: *I'm not. I found something that just didn't make sense. Listen to this, 'Slippery food is held in the mouth by* **minute** (pupil pronounces word as in 60 seconds to a **minute**) *teeth.' That doesn't make sense.* Teacher: *It is excellent that you realised that it doesn't make sense. What did you do?* Pupil 2: *I went back and read it again, and it still didn't make sense.* Teacher: *Let's forget the actual word for a moment. Will you read the sentence again and just leave a gap when you come to that word.* Pupil 2: *'Slippery food is held in the mouth by – teeth.'* Teacher: *What sort of a word should it be?*

Objective	Sample dialogue
	Pupil 2: *It should tell me about the teeth.* Teacher: *Don't worry about the exact word, just suggest a few words that would make sense.* Pupil: *Sharp...white...little...* Teacher: *You're nearly there.*
Year 1, Term 1, Word Level 12: Acquisition of new words from reading; making collections of personal interest or significant words and words linked to particular topics. Reception, Word Level, 10 & 11 Year 1, Term 2, Word Level 10 Year 1, Term 3, Word Level 8 Year 2, Term 1, Word Level 10 Year 2, Term 2, Word Level 10 Year 2, Term 3, Word Level 9 Year 1, Term 2, Text Level 20: To use simple dictionaries, and to understand their alphabetical organisation. Year 2, Term 2, Text Level 16 & 17: To use dictionaries and glossaries to locate words... That dictionaries and glossaries give definitions and explanations... Explore some simple definitions in dictionaries.	Teacher: *Did anybody find any words they would like to put into their word books?* Pupil 1: *I did. I found two – habitat and reproduction.* Teacher: *Why did you choose those?* Pupil 1: *Because we talked about them before we started to read and I didn't know them before, but when I came to them in the book I could read them and know what they meant.* Pupil 2: *I found 'amphibian'.* Teacher: *What does it mean?* Pupil 2: *I'm not sure. Does it mean it sleeps in the day and wakes up at night?* Teacher: *Let's find it in the text and read it again to see if we can work it out... Now we'll check what we've decided by looking in the dictionary... Do you know, there's another way we could have found out about that word, and we didn't think of it? Can anybody make a suggestion?* Pupil 3: *We could have looked in the back of the book at that sort of index, look, here...* Teacher: *Well done! Yes, we could have looked in the glossary – that's what it's called. Everybody turn to the glossary on page 24...* Pupil 4: *I found 'hibernation' and I thought it meant sleeping. Can I check in the glossary to make sure?* Teacher: *Good idea. Let's all have a look for 'hibernation' in the glossary...*

Objective	Sample dialogue
Year 1, Term 3, Text Level 19: To locate parts of the text that give particular information, including labelled diagrams and charts. Year 2, Term 2, Text Level 19: To read flow charts and cyclical diagrams that explain a process.	Teacher: *Who has found out the answer to our question 'What is frogspawn and how does it turn into frogs?'* Pupil 1: *I know. The female sheds her eggs...* Teacher: *Well done. Now, can you tell me where you found this information?* Pupil 1: *I read it right here* (points). Teacher: *That's very good. Tell me, did anyone else get some information another way?* Pupil 2: *I did. I found this diagram that shows how the frogspawn turns into tadpoles, then the tadpoles turn into frogs. It's here, on page 5. Look, it's labelled so you can tell what is happening.* Teacher: *Would you stand up and show everyone the diagram and tell us how you understood what it was telling you?*

It is not essential that the group as a whole reach consensus on any points of discussion, but it is important that claims can be supported by reference to the text. Children also need to be shown that some answers to questions will require their background knowledge as well as what is stated in the text.

The teacher links this discussion to the next section of text by encouraging pupils to:

- ask a question about the next section of text
- find the answer to a question.

After Reading

An effective guided reading session culminates in a review of the initial reason for reading. After the final section of text has been considered, the group returns to the original purpose for the reading and summarises their thoughts *(Year 2, Term 3, Text Level 18: To evaluate the usefulness of a text for its purpose).*

- Do you think that this book answered most of our questions?
- Did you find it interesting?
- What did you learn about...?

They make comparisons with other texts on the same topic *(Year 1, Term 3, Text Level 17: To recognise that non-fiction books on similar themes can give different information and present similar information in different ways).*

- Did you feel that this book was as useful as the one we read yesterday on frogs?
- What did you find out from this book that was not in yesterday's book?
- Did you find both books equally easy or difficult to understand?
- Which book did you think had the best photos and diagrams?
- The two books had different features in them didn't they? What did you think about the glossary (index, footnotes...)?

The teacher encourages motivation to undertake associated reading.

- Yusuf, you were saying that you still hadn't found out exactly what happens to frogs when they hibernate. I've put a pile of other books about frogs on the table if you, or anybody else, wants to find out some more.

The summary of the session also provides an opportunity to lead pupils into an activity or into the class reflection session.

- Let's think for a couple of minutes of what we want to share with the rest of the class. Remember that they haven't had the chance to read this particular text. We can tell them about some facts we have learned, or something about the useful features that we found in the book.

- Later on we're going to make mind-maps about frogs and then compare them with the brainstorming sheet we constructed before we began to read. It will be interesting to see all the new information we have learned.

Selecting the text for the next guided reading session can also take place.

- Next week we're going to be thinking about snakes. I've got some books here that might be good. Let's have a quick preview and see if we like the look of one more than another.

Reading – Section 2

Using Fiction in a Guided Reading Session

Before Reading
Discussion Guide

Objective	Sample dialogue
Year 1, Term 1, Text Level 7: To use titles, cover pages, pictures and 'blurbs' to predict the content of unfamiliar stories. Year 1, Term 1, Text Level 5: To describe story settings...	Teacher: *What sort of a book do you think this is?* Pupil 1: *It's about frogs.* Teacher: *Do you think it's like the book we've just finished on frogs?* Pupil 1: *No.* Teacher: *Why not?* Pupil 1: *Well, the frogs have got clothes on and they're talking to each other.* Teacher: *So it's not non-fiction.* Pupil 1: *No, it's fiction.* Pupil 2: *I knew that because I could see it's by Arnold Lobel. He writes lovely stories about Frog and Toad. I love them.* Pupil 3: *Yes, and anyway, look at the title 'Frog and Toad are Friends'. That's a story title, not non-fiction.* Teacher: *Where do you think Frog and Toad live?* Pupil 4: *They live in their own little houses. Look, here's a picture of one, and they go out to play in the country. See, here they are by the river...*
Year 1, Term 3, Text Level 8: To compare and contrast stories with a variety of settings.	Teacher: *I'm glad Ahmed likes Frog and Toad stories, how do the rest of you feel?* Pupil 1: *I liked that story we read last week about the little girl in India. I like stories about children who live in other countries.* Teacher: *Why do you like those especially?* Pupil 1: *Because they're like the stories my Mum tells me about when she was a little girl in India.* Pupil 4: *I like stories about dinosaurs, because they're not real and they're fun.* Pupil 5: *I like fairy stories like the Gingerbread Man because we can do puppets afterwards...*

Before Reading

Objective	Sample dialogue
Year 2, Term 1, Text Level 3: To be aware of the difference between spoken and written language...	Teacher: *As you read this story, I want you to notice when the words or sentences are just right for a written story, but would sound funny if you used them when you were talking to each other.* Pupil: *Like Once upon a time, or Happily ever after?* Teacher: *Yes, just like that.*

During Reading
Discussion Guide

Objective	Sample dialogue
Year 1, Term 1, Text Level 1 & 2, and all subsequent Year Levels and Terms: To reinforce and apply their word-level skills... To use phonological, contextual, grammatical and graphic knowledge to work out, predict and check the meanings of unfamiliar words and to make sense of what they read.	Pupil: *I don't know what this word is.* Teacher: *Read the sentence through and leave a gap where the word is.* Pupil: *All the ——— were closed.* Teacher: *Now read the sentence before as well.* Pupil: *It was dark. All the ——— were closed.* Teacher: *What would make sense?* Pupil: *Doors, but it doesn't start with 'd'.* Teacher: *What else might be closed?* Pupil: *Windows.* Teacher: *But the windows would still let the light in, unless...* Pupil: *The curtains were drawn!* Teacher: *Well done, you're very close. Now divide the word into two and see if you can read it.* Pupil: *Sh-ut, shut. E-r-s, ers. Shutters! What are they?* Teacher: *What do you think they might be?* Pupil: *Sort of curtains that shut...*
Year 1, Term 1, Text Level 3: Notice the difference between spoken and written forms. Year 1, Term 2, Text Level 5: To identify some key features of story language...	Pupil 1: *I've found something I wouldn't say!* Teacher: *What?* Pupil 1: *'The clear, warm light of April'. I'd never say that!* Pupil 2: *And I've found 'We will skip through the meadows.' I'd never say that either!* Teacher: *Why wouldn't you say it?*

Objective	Sample dialogue
	Pupil 1: *It sounds a bit like poetry. You'd never talk about the clear, warm light of April. Your Mum might say, 'It's a lovely, sunny April day.' It's all right in the book, but you'd sound stupid saying it.*
Year 1, Term 2, Text Level 7: To discuss reasons for, or causes of, incidents in stories.	Teacher: *Why do you think Toad refused to get up?* Pupil 1: *He just didn't want to get out of bed.* Pupil 2: *Perhaps he hates getting up in the morning.* Teacher: *Think of what we know about toads and frogs, and the clues we've been given in the beginning of the story...* Pupil 3: *I know, they've been hibernating, We know it's been winter because Frog says, 'The snow is melting,' and 'It is spring!'. No wonder Toad doesn't want to get up!* Teacher: *Well done – you're very clever to remember what we've been learning about hibernation. How did Frog get him up in the end?* Pupil 4: *Frog made the calender say 'May'.* Teacher: *And was it really May?* Pupil 5: *Not really, because look, Frog had just been talking about the clear, warm light of April!*
Year 2, Term 1, Text Level 6: To discuss familiar story themes and link to own experiences, e.g. illness...	Pupil 1: *I like this story. Toad is so nice to Frog as he's not feeling well.* Teacher: *That's the one good thing about being ill, everyone makes a fuss of you!* Pupil 2: *When I had my tonsils out, nobody told me to eat up the things I hate!* Pupil 3: *I made my Mum a cup of tea when she was resting before the new baby came.* Pupil 4: *And my Dad told me lots of stories about when he was little. He was much better than Toad at thinking of stories...*

Objective	Sample dialogue
Year 1, Term 2, Text Level 8: To identify and discuss characters, e.g. appearance, behaviour, qualities: to speculate about how they might behave; to discuss how they are described in the text; and to compare characters from different stories.	Teacher: *Do you think Frog and Toad are like different people or are they much the same?* Pupil 1: *I think they're quite different. Frog's got much more, more...* Teacher: *Oomph?* Pupil 1: *Yes, oomph. He's much quicker and he's got more go. He's always a bit ahead of Toad.* Pupil 2: *But he's very kind and always wants to help Toad.* Pupil 3: *Toad's kind too – look how hard he tried to think of a story to tell Frog when he wasn't well...*
Year 2, Term 3, Text Level 7: To compare stories by same author: settings, characters, themes, to evaluate and form preferences, giving reasons.	Teacher: *So now we've read five Frog and Toad stories. Which one did you like the best?* Pupil 1: *I like them all. I like them because they're so ordinary, somehow. I mean, nothing much happens, but they're just really nice.* Teacher: *What about the settings?* Pupil 1: *That's just what I mean. They're all in the same setting, the same houses and countryside – you feel you know it as if you've been there.* Pupil 2: *And Frog and Toad are always the same, nice to each other, and funny.* Pupil 3: *I like the stories because I know I'm going to like them.* Teacher: *Would you always like stories that you feel safe with? I mean, you seemed to enjoy the Roald Dahl stories I've been reading to you...* Pupil 4: *Oh, they're different. I like them for different reasons. Everybody is weird and some people are horrible and you never know where they're going to end up or what's going to happen next.* Pupil 5: *I like the Frog and Toad stories because they're sort of comfortable, but I like the Roald Dahl stories because they're not!*

After Reading

An effective guided reading session culminates in a review of the reading, with a focus on the main objective or goal for reading. After the final section of text has been read, the group summarises their thoughts and discusses strategies and understandings that have been considered during the reading.

Such a summary would include:

- An assessment of the worth or enjoyment derived from the text:
  - Why do you think we all enjoyed this story so much?
  - Did you like the ending? Was it a surprise?
- A judgement of whether the reading purpose was achieved:
  - We were going to find some examples that show the difference between story language and the language we use when we talk to each other. Let's think about what we came up with and why we decided the language was different.
  - One of our main purposes in reading was to try and use the read-on, leave a gap and re-read strategy to help us when we found a word we couldn't read or didn't understand. Let's talk about how we did it and whether it worked for us.
- A motivation to undertake associated independent reading:
  - I've put some more stories by Arnold Lobel on the table for anyone who wants to spend some more time with Frog and Toad. There are also some other stories that are quite different about frogs and toads – you may like to read them and see which you like best.
- Choosing a follow-up activity:
  - On that shelf you'll find all the stories that we've read this term. On the shelf underneath there are some stories we haven't read yet. I'd like you to look through them and consider all the story beginnings and see which make you want to read on, and which don't. We'll make a collection of story beginnings and sort them into two piles. After that we'll try and see why some are so appealing and others are not *(Year 1, Term 2, Text Level 10: To identify and compare basic story elements, e.g. beginnings and endings in different stories)*.
  - Other follow-up activities could include making a story map, constructing a simple sociogram, Readers' Theatre, putting on a puppet show, re-telling the story in a variety of ways, innovating on the text or conducting character interviews.
- Selecting a text for the next guided reading session:
  - I think we've probably read enough Frog and Toad stories for now. What would you like to read next? I thought some poetry might be a good idea, so I've chosen some really fabulous anthologies about Monsters and Dragons and Dinosaurs as well as Diabolical Children. Have a look through this pile and we'll choose one for next Thursday.

- Collecting or comparing elements of text – as children participate in a number of guided reading sessions they collect, classify and discuss elements from different texts. A large class chart could be constructed, listing elements and adding relevant comments and illustrations. Elements could include:

    - Textual features such as the type of narrative, e.g. fairy tale, traditional stories from different cultures, adventure, fantasy, plays, humorous poems, lyrical poems, poems from different lands
    - Story settings, types of characters, plot structures
    - Opening and/or closing sentences
    - Common ways of introducing and concluding dialogue: *said, replied, asked, shrieked, gasped, howled, muttered*
    - Themes
    - Authors
    - Descriptive phrases that appeal for one reason or another.

These elements are gradually built up by the children to form a powerful resource for them to call on when they need it as writers. The process of analysing texts helps children to build up understandings about authors, narratives and the power of the written word that is extended and deepened as they move through the school.

Reciprocal Reading

Another form of guided reading is known as **Reciprocal Reading**.

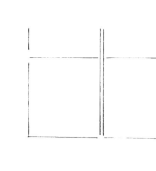

What is Reciprocal Reading?

This technique was described by Palincsar and Brown in 1985 and has been widely used, with great success, since that time.

- 'Reciprocal' refers to the way in which the teacher and pupil change roles and teach each other to answer different types of questions.
- Initially the teacher models the process, demonstrating the use of a charted framework to direct the lesson.
- The teacher models the different types of questions and how to answer and substantiate them from the text. Only one or two types of question, focusing on the objective of the session, are taught in any one session.
- Pupils take turns at being the teacher in questioning and substantiating answers from the text.

Reading – Section 2

| **What Does it Do?** | - It caters for readers who have reached the Early Phase and beyond.
- It involves the pupil as teacher and learner.
- It teaches the reading comprehension strategies of predicting, questioning, summarising, and clarifying.
- It teaches pupils to construct their own questions.
- It teaches children to understand texts at different levels.
- It teaches pupils to substantiate their opinions by referring to appropriate portions of text and by linking these to their own experience.
- It provides opportunity for children to practise word identification strategies.
- It is interactive and collaborative.
- It is effective in a small group teaching situation with pupils of mixed abilities. |
|---|---|
| **Does it Help Children Experiencing Difficulty with Reading?** | Reciprocal reading is an effective strategy to use with these children because they are supported in their reading by the use of:
- the set framework which guides the lesson;
- the articulation and modelling of strategies used by good readers when reading;
- by hearing peers asking questions and seeking clarification on difficult words in the text;
- by increased opportunity for interaction with the teacher and other group members;
- by repeated demonstrations of the different levels of questioning and substantiation from the text. |
| **What Do I need?** | Reciprocal reading involves a small group of children (not more than eight) and requires:
- a copy of the selected text for each pupil
- charted copies of the set questions that form the framework of the lesson. |
| **How Do I Do It?** | **Before Reading**
- Explain the teaching/learning strategy, i.e. Reciprocal Reading and its purpose.
- Explain the lesson objective, i.e. the specific reading strategy or process that is going to be learned.
- Activate background knowledge and relate it to the specific text being used. |

- Choose a leader. Initially this will be the teacher, but subsequently, when children are familiar with the process, the leader can be one of the children. In the early stages of using this strategy the pupil chosen needs to be a volunteer or one confident of his/her ability. The teacher and remaining children guide and support the leader as necessary.

During Reading

Follow the charted lesson framework to teach and practise the strategies of:

- questioning
- clarifying
- predicting
- summarising.

After Reading

- Revisit the lesson objective.

- Reflect on progress made towards the achievement of the objective, and relate this to previous and ongoing learning.

- Give pupils opportunities to practise the reading strategy taught independently.

- Provide opportunities for children to have additional practice using activities such as story grammar, cause and effect, change the point of view, and character interviews. These can be found in the *First Steps* book in this series *Fiction and Poetry at Key Stage 1*.

Reciprocal reading framework

Predicting (New Text)	<ul><li>Use titles, pictures, experience to make predictions.</li><li>Ask group to discuss your predictions.</li><li>Ask group to read first part of text (approximately one or two paragraphs).</li></ul>
Clarifying	<ul><li>Ask the group to identify words and phrases that are not understood.</li><li>Ask group to help by using context clues and picture cues.</li><li>If word remains unknown teacher clarifies.</li></ul>
Questioning	<ul><li>Ask questions: Literal – answer is in the text Inferential – answer can be found 'between the lines' Evaluative – answer can be drawn from the child's own experience.</li><li>Choose children to answer.</li><li>Ask children to answer question and discuss answer.</li><li>Ask children to evaluate question type.</li></ul>
Summarising	<ul><li>Summarise what group has read.</li><li>Be brief and cover main points only.</li><li>Ask group to change or add to your summary if necessary.</li></ul>
Predicting	<ul><li>Predict what you think the next segment will be about.</li><li>Use last sentence, headings, pictures, own experiences.</li><li>Discuss predictions with group.</li><li>Choose another leader. (Repeat Questioning. Continue cycle of questioning, clarifying, summarising.)</li></ul>

Independent Reading

Children at all levels of development need opportunities to read independently on a daily basis. Independent reading time allows them to learn to read by reading and provides opportunities for them to:

- practise the knowledge, skills and understandings they are learning;
- select texts and read for enjoyment;
- re-read texts they have worked on in teaching sessions;
- focus on specific reading strategies that may have been targeted for improved performance;
- choose texts written by a favourite author or of a particular genre.

Teachers encourage the desire to read by establishing positive attitudes to reading through:

- making learning successful
- sharing favourite texts
- engaging children in 'story' through daily reading aloud class serials
- providing opportunities for sharing responses to texts with peers, parents and teacher
- modelling and valuing independent reading
- providing a wide variety of high quality texts of different types.

Independent reading can be practised in a range of class contexts. Teachers and children choose those best suited to their situation. Teachers discuss with their pupils the purpose/s for reading, and focus explicitly on the reading strategies that are used before, during and after reading.

Uninterrupted Silent Sustained Reading

Time is put aside each day to allow puils at least 10 minutes of independent reading time. Children select their own text, reading silently for the allocated time. Children in the Role Play Phase can quietly look at picture books or books with minimal print, 'telling themselves the story'. At the end of reading time children may reflect on and share their response to the text in some way. This response could take the form of a journal entry; sharing within a small group; spontaneously drawing or composing; or having a whole class reading conference with the teacher.

Paired Reading

This independent reading strategy can be used within one class, or it can be used across classes and year levels. Children select a book they wish to read and share with a partner or 'buddy'. They choose their book with consideration for their own and their 'buddy's' interests and ability, and the text's appeal. Time is then organised for children to practise their reading, and then to share their text with their 'buddy'. The strategy may or may not be used on a regular basis, with the same or changing partners.

Readers' Circle

Children read a chosen text independently. They read whenever they like, for example, at home, in a designated reading time, or when they finish a task early. They use removable stickers to note their comments and questions as they read. Children and teacher then meet once a week in a small group situation to share their reading of the text. During the session the teacher and children ask the questions and discuss the issues that arose from their reading of the text. As they know they will be challenged to share their critical questioning, thinking and responding to the text, children read more deeply than they might otherwise have done.

In his book *Tell Me – Children, Reading and Talk* (1993, The Thimble Press), Aiden Chambers suggests that teachers use a framework for discussing texts, beginning by asking children what they liked/disliked in the text, leading on to what patterns they noticed and what puzzles they found. He describes how children quickly move away from the like/dislike questions, preferring the patterns and puzzles. At the end of each Readers' Circle session children process the information discussed using a mind map, reflective journal, plot profile, etc.

Reading Bags

In this strategy, the teacher organises a Reading Bag to take home, containing a selection of approximately eight to 10 reading texts. The texts are chosen to be appealing and appropriate to the reading levels of the children. Pupils take turns to take the Reading Bag home for a designated time. It is important to allow children time to read and enjoy the texts. Books in the Reading Bag are quite different from those that children may read for homework. If at all possible, when budgets allow, books should be specially purchased for the bag. Where this is not possible, library books could be used. Children are encouraged to share their enjoyment with parents. When the bag is returned to school, time is provided for each child to share reflections and responses to their reading experience.

WRITING

The importance of writing is increasingly being acknowledged, not only as a major aspect of literacy in itself, but as a significant factor in learning to read. The understandings that children construct as writers greatly illuminate their awareness of words and structures as readers. A Literacy Hour does not allow a great deal of time for individual independent writing, although it provides a wonderful opportunity to enable children to enter into a writer's mind through modelled and shared writing. Teachers need to ensure that many opportunities are given to children to put into practice what they have learned in these sessions when they write independently and purposefully in other subject areas.

Modelled Writing

What is Modelled Writing?

Modelled writing is a simple but powerful strategy that can be used to teach the concepts, skills and strategies of writing. The teacher stands in front of the class, equipped with a writing implement and a large, highly visible, writing surface, such as a blackboard or flip-chart, explicitly demonstrating how thoughts become written words. When the teacher adopts the role of author and wrestles with the writing of a text for a real purpose and audience, thinking aloud as each challenge is confronted and met, pupils are able to see into the mind of a skilled writer. Pupils are privy to where ideas come from, how sentences are formed, why they need editing, how paragraphs are formed and a range of other tricks of the writer's trade.

Why Model Writing Strategies?

Like reading, writing is an intangible process for many children. It is essential that teachers make explicit the many ways in which writers go about writing. Modelled writing:

- provides explicit demonstrations of writing strategies and the writing process;
- builds pupils' knowledge about the English language, including the structure and features of different text types;
- shows how reading and writing are related;
- encourages pupils to analyse and assess writing;
- shows how writing can be shaped for different purposes and different audiences;
- gives EAL pupils access to the writing process and shows them how English is written;
- demonstrates the importance of writing as a form of communication;
- helps pupils hear, build up and use a language to talk about writing.

When Do I Use Modelled Writing?

Modelled writing is best conducted immediately before pupils are expected to apply the strategies modelled. Within the Literacy Hour, the first 10 to 15 minutes is normally allocated to shared reading or writing. It may be possible to conduct a modelled writing session that leads into shared reading or shared writing, taking about 15 to 20 minutes in all.

In Key Stage 1, modelled writing sessions need to be short and intensive. Often it is quite sufficient to model the writing of one sentence, illustrating one major concept or strategy. It is appropriate to do this in the context of the Literacy Hour, to provide a dynamic and explicit illustration of the strategy or skill that is the focus of the hour. It is also entirely appropriate to seize on any opportunity that arises during the day to provide further consolidation of a chosen objective. For instance, a teacher might model:

- the writing of a note that will go home to parents;
- the writing of a message that can be delivered to another teacher;
- the writing of a list of items that are needed from the shop;
- the writing of simple instructions for a craft lesson;
- the writing of a greetings card;
- the writing of a thank-you letter.

All of these instances illustrate an important point – that modelled writing in Key Stage 1 needs to be highly focused, relevant and short.

If a small group of pupils is experiencing difficulty with a particular aspect of writing, a teacher might be able to create an opportunity to work with this group for a short time while modelling a piece of writing that meets their particular need. This time could be 'stolen' from the beginning of the time allocated for small group work in the Literacy Hour. An explicit demonstration of a specific strategy in action in a relevant context provides a perfect springboard for pupils to write independently, using the strategy that has just been demonstrated.

Although a modelled writing session is a complete entity in itself, it is critical that the objective of the session has a real connection to another task. Children need to see the purpose of the modelling, and have an opportunity to apply their learned knowledge and/or skill in a context that is relevant for them.

How Do I Choose my Objective?

Objectives for modelled writing are drawn from three inter-related areas. These are:

- the processes of writing
- writing skills and strategies
- writing concepts or knowledge.

The following chart provides examples of aspects of each area. Only one or two aspects would form the focus of a session.

Writing process	Concepts/knowledge: purposes, structures and features of text forms	Concepts/knowledge: conventions	Skills and strategies
Role Play and Experimental Phases Determining purpose, audience and text form needed Generating ideas Soliciting ideas Re-reading and Revising as writing proceeds Checking when finished	*Role Play and Experimental Phases* Nursery rhymes Simple poems/rhymes Labels/signs/captions Simple instructions Recounts Simple reports Greetings cards Simple letters/notes A simple serialised story	*Role Play and Experimental Phases* Directionality Concepts of print Symbol/sound correspondence Alphabetic and phonic knowledge	*Role Play and Experimental Phases* Word choice and use Spelling Sentence construction Handwriting Organisation
Early Phase Determining purpose, audience and text form Generating ideas Gathering information Drafting and rewriting as an ongoing process Soliciting ideas Conferencing Revising Editing Proof reading Publishing Sharing	*Early Phase* Letters/faxes/email Recount Explanation Description Simple report Simple narrative (serialised) Summaries Poetry of different types	*Early Phase* Spelling Critical features of words Grammar including - sentence structure - use of words/word classes - punctuation - specific language features Layout and presentation	*Early Phase* Sentence construction and manipulation Spelling Organisation

The *First Steps* Literacy Developmental Continuum helps teachers identify where pupils are in terms of their literacy development and provides a list of Major Teaching Emphases appropriate for each element of writing. The National Literacy Strategy Programme of Teaching Objectives provides a structure of progression for the required range of work. By accessing these two documents and using the in-head knowledge of the strengths and weaknesses of the class or group, teachers are able to choose an objective that will meet the needs of their pupils. For example:

- *Literacy Developmental Continuum:* Experimental Phase Indicator 10 – understands and experiments with significant punctuation in context, e.g. full stops, capital letters

- *Literacy Developmental Continuum:* Experimental Phase Major Teaching Emphasis 10 – continue to model the use of simple punctuation, such as full stops, capital letters and question marks

- *National Literacy Strategy Programme of Objectives:* Year 1, Term 1, Sentence Level 8 & 9 – to begin to use full stops to demarcate sentences; to use a capital letter for the personal pronoun 'I' and for the start of a sentence.

Are Pupils Grouped?

Usually in Key Stage 1 the whole class is included in modelled writing sessions. All are extended at their own level of competency. The major objective is chosen because nearly all children need to learn a particular concept, process or strategy. If a few children know this already, their understanding will be refined and extended. All children take from a modelled writing session whatever they are capable of learning at any given time.

What Resources Will I Need?

Modelled writing sessions are usually conducted using a flip-chart or board, so that pupils can see what the teacher is doing very clearly. If a flip-chart or large sheet of paper is used, this provides a permanent record of the proceedings. If the paper is left on display, pupils can return to it and recall the concept or skill that was demonstrated.

If teachers model the use of references as an aid to writing, such as a word bank or class chart, these should be available for the children to use when they are writing themselves. Modelled writing provides an excellent vehicle for modelling the effective use of resources.

What is the Role of the Teacher?

In modelled writing, the teacher's role is one of:

- motivating pupils to write
- reading aloud the text that is being written recursively and expressively
- thinking aloud about the targeted skill or strategy (objective)
- demonstrating how writers construct meaning for a purpose and audience.

How Does Modelled Writing Work?

If the modelled writing session is to be either one of a series or part of a unit of work, consideration should be given as to what part this context plays in the larger plan. For example, a focus on a particular text form, such as a recount, could warrant a sequence of lessons familiarising pupils with the structure and features of that text form. Further information is given about this in the *First Steps* book *Information Texts at Key Stage 1*.

Before writing, it is valuable to explain to pupils what objective will be taught and why. (*We all enjoyed the visit of that nice police officer, so I thought it would be a good idea if we wrote to thank her. Soon you can write your own letter, but I thought I'd write mine first so that you could see how I set it out*). This also includes a clear statement of the intended purpose and audience.

Prior to the modelled writing session, it could also be appropriate to draw from the pupils all they already know about the concept, skill, strategy or process. For example: '*Has anyone seen this punctuation mark before? Where did you see it, Rashed? What did you think it meant? Do you know what it is called? Does anyone know?*'

Each action carried out by the teacher is accompanied by a think-aloud explanation: *'I'm going to make a list of things I need to make my cake. I'll write the words one below the other, so that I can read them easily and tick them off as I go. I need flour – fl-our, butter – but-ter, sugar – that's funny, it sounds like "sh", but there's no "h" in sugar, eggs – e-gg-s, chocolate – choc-o-late'* or *'Now, I need to think of a word that tells how scared I was when the big dog jumped out on me. I was...frightened... that doesn't sound half as bad as I felt... scared stiff... that sounds all right, but perhaps "absolutely terrified" sounds the way I felt. Yes, I'll put "absolutely terrified". Now, how do I spell "absolutely"? a-b-s-ol-ute-ly. Later I might check that word in the dictionary...'*

As modelled writing sessions generally only run for five or six minutes in Key Stage 1, the objective is clearly focused upon and demonstrated with clearly worded explanations.

After modelling, it is important to review the main teaching points by re-reading the text and thinking aloud about the impact of the objective on what has been written. For example, *'After reading my recount through again, I'm sure that people who read it will know how very, very scared I was because the words I chose will make them understand.'*

Shared or independent writing provides a purposeful sequel to modelled writing because pupils have the opportunity to apply their understandings. If a shared reading session follows modelled writing, it is important that attention is drawn to the features in the text that mirror the objective of the modelled writing.

After the writing has been finished, teachers can:

- leave the writing on display for frequent reference or as a focus for discussion;

- publish the piece of writing or use it in context, e.g. a notice for the classroom door telling parents about a coming event;

- use the writing as the basis for a range of reading activities, for example, cloze, text innovation, text reconstruction;

- collate copies of writing for future reference. For example: *'Can you find the piece of modelled writing we did when we were thinking about capital letters? Let's use it to remind ourselves of the rules.'*

Shared Writing

What is Shared Writing?

Shared writing provides a context that encourages pupils to apply their understandings about writing within a supportive environment, free from the burden of responsibility of being the sole author. The teacher stands in front of the class, equipped with a writing implement and a large writing surface, such as a whiteboard or flip-chart, just as in modelled writing. The major difference lies in the role played by the pupils. In modelled writing, the teacher is in total control of the process. The explicit demonstration of a chosen aspect of writing is unashamedly didactic. Pupils might make suggestions and pose questions, but the focus is on the teacher's demonstration. In shared writing, the reason for writing is distinctly different. The aim is for the class and the teacher to combine their efforts to produce a joint piece of writing. The role of the teacher is more one of scribe and motivator, rather than writer-in-charge. The thought processes, the decisions and the resultant writing belong to the whole class, not just the teacher.

Why Use Shared Writing Strategies?

Writing places multiple demands on a writer. When a writer needs to come to terms with an unfamiliar or challenging aspect of writing – a difficult audience, an unfamiliar text form or a specific purpose that is daunting – the process often becomes formidable. Developing writers need to be freed from the demands of writing when they are trying to apply new understandings, skills, strategies and processes. Shared writing:

- provides opportunities for developing writers to use and consolidate new learning;
- enables the teacher and pupils to experience the writing process together;
- provides a testing ground on which pupils can experiment with what they are learning;
- allows pupils to gain confidence as part of collective authorship;
- provides a forum for pupils to discuss and evaluate what makes effective writing;
- provides total support for EAL pupils confronted by the demands of written English;
- helps pupils build up and use a language to talk about writing.

When Do I Use Shared Writing?

In Key Stage 1, teachers often seize unexpected opportunities as they arise to model the writing of a very short text. In the same way they grasp at many incidental opportunities to share writing with children. Shared writing is an excellent way of enabling children to put into practice something they have seen the teacher model very recently. For instance, a teacher might model the writing of a shopping list, focusing on the list form and on particular graphophonic relationships. Later on, the class might be asked to send a list of stationery requirements to the office – this time children and teacher would share the writing of the list, applying and practising what had just been learned.

It can also be very profitable to conduct an intensive series of shared writing sessions designed to reinforce objectives undertaken previously in modelled writing. Such sessions might focus on a particular form of text. The sessions would provide opportunities for pupils to contribute to the writing of a more sustained piece of text. The outcome of a draft piece of writing is then achieved over a number of sessions, instead of one short, intensive lesson. There is great value in having pupils contribute to a piece of writing as it grows and is re-shaped over time. When a teacher and pupils complete a joint piece of writing and present it to the intended audience for feedback, they complete the writing process.

How Do I Choose my Objective?

If a modelled writing session consists of a short, intensive focus on an immediately relevant writing task, then the main objective may well be chosen from the Sentence and Word Levels. In Key Stage 1 children are coming to terms with basic sentence structure and need to be given every possible opportunity to put their growing understandings to work in a supportive context. Young children are also grappling with concepts of print, for instance, that a spoken word can be represented in print and that a written word consists of a block of letters with space on either side. They also need to apply their growing knowledge of the relationships between sounds and letters as often as possible. Shared writing offers an excellent opportunity for this to happen.

Shared writing also provides an opportunity to share the conscious, explicit use of a specific writing strategy. Not only does this teach children why and how a strategy is used, but also it provides a context in which to explain the choices and decisions that are constantly made by writers.

One of the primary aims of shared writing is also to teach pupils how to deal with the entire writing process. In order to achieve this, some shared writing sessions need to be much longer and more comprehensive than others. Where possible, the writing tasks should be real or lifelike. It is important that each session, or sequence of sessions, needs to represent an authentic writing experience.

Inevitably, the major objective for a sequence of shared writing lessons is taken from the Text Level, and involves the teaching of purpose, structure and features of a specific text form. Objectives from the Sentence and Word Levels are also taught, but these usually represent Word or Sentence Level features of the chosen text type.

A teaching sequence might be as follows:

Familiarisation stage	1	The teacher models the writing of a series of oral recounts. These could be derived from children's 'Show and Tell' or 'News' sessions at the beginning of the school day. They might also represent personal recounts drawn from the teacher's experiences.
	2	Texts written by the teacher in modelled writing sessions are used for shared reading. Published texts can also be used. Texts need to be short and they need to vary in quality, which is why it is sometimes easier if they are constructed by the teacher.
Problem-solving stage	1	Children compare the quality of the texts that have been read. Discussion focuses on whether or not the texts provide readers with essential information.
	2	Children, either in small groups or as a whole class, rank the texts in order of merit, giving reasons for their choice. For instance, do the writers provide vital information relating to when and where an incident took place, who participated and what was the sequence of events and outcome?
	3	A chart is constructed that sets out the elements of a good recount, as deduced by the children.
Testing the hypothesis	1	The teacher models or shares the reading of some more recounts, using the chart as a framework by which the quality of the recounts is measured.
	2	The framework is amended or extended if this is judged to be necessary by the children.
Using the framework in a shared writing session		Teacher and children use the framework they have constructed as the basis for writing a class recount.

As the teacher uses the framework in preparation for a shared writing session, talk is focused on the content and structure of the recount. This sets the scene, through planning, for the writing that follows. At various points during the actual writing of the recount, discussion might centre on some of the following:

- the choice of words, including graphic adjectives and verbs;

- the ways in which the words could be structured to form sentences, focusing especially on conjunctions of time, which are so essential in a recount;

- the ways in which a sentence can be manipulated for better effect;

- the need for subject/verb and noun/pronoun agreement (in a very informal and highly contextualised way);
- the use of phonics as a spelling strategy, focusing especially on the phonic element;
- the helpfulness of having a large bank of words that can be spelt 'without thinking about it';
- any other objective that needs to be covered at the Word, Sentence or Text Level.

Of course, only one or two of these objectives that are mutually supportive would be chosen for any one session. It is very important that due consideration is given to the demands being made on the working memory, because if it is overloaded then children will be unable to learn effectively. All of these objectives will need to be revisited frequently over time. If sufficient familiarisation has taken place, and if children have contributed to the problem-solving session/s that followed, then the teaching/learning process becomes an affirmation of children's growing understandings rather than a struggle with new information.

Using the Literacy Continuum to Support Teaching Objectives

The *First Steps* Literacy Continuum helps teachers identify where pupils are in terms of their literacy development and provides a list of appropriate Major Teaching Emphases that are linked to Phases of Development in each element of writing. The Programme of Teaching Objectives provides a structure of progression for the required range of work. By accessing these two documents, teachers are able to choose objectives that will meet the needs of their pupils. For example:

- *Literacy Developmental Continuum:* Experimental Phase Indicator 6 – assumes that a reader shares the context so may not give sufficient background information, e.g. may tell 'who' but not 'when'
- *Literacy Developmental Continuum:* Experimental Phase, Major Teaching Emphasis 6 – continue to model and share personal and other daily writing with children, extending understanding of purpose and audience, basic language structures, fundamental language features
- *National Literacy Strategy Programme of Teaching Objectives:* Reception Year, Text Level 15 – to use writing to communicate in a variety of ways, incorporating it into play and everyday classroom life, e.g. recounting their own experiences, lists, signs, directions…

Are Pupils Grouped?

Shared writing is normally conducted with an entire class. The benefits of sharing ideas and understandings are greatest when a range of pupils are participating. Weaker writers gain an insight into how the more skilled writers of the group manage the multiple demands of writing.

What Resources Will I Need?	Like modelled writing, shared writing sessions need to be conducted so that all the children can see clearly what is happening so that they can share in the task of composition. During the session, pupils are encouraged to use all available resources such as class-constructed charts of a specific text form and class word-banks.
What is my Role?	In shared writing the teacher's role is one of: - motivating pupils; - alerting pupils to the decisions writers make, for example, *'So shall we begin our story with "Once upon a time...", as suggested by Kerry, or "Long, long ago...", as suggested by Ross?';* - guiding the writing of the text by facilitating discussion, for example, *'Do you think we should start our recount with when, or who?';* - inviting participation from as many pupils as possible.
How Does Shared Writing Work?	Shared writing sessions are the ideal context to help pupils move from the explicit demonstration of modelled writing to the relative independence of guided writing. Whereas modelled writing can be used to demonstrate a specific concept or skill and connect it to the writing task, shared writing is better suited to a sequence of lessons which culminates in a complete piece of writing. Before writing, the teacher tells the children the reason for the shared writing. For example, *'The Year 2 class have heard that we had a fantastic expedition to the fire station. They are wondering if they would like to go themselves. I said that we'd write an account of our visit to help them make up their minds.'* Before beginning the writing, the teacher asks the pupils what they think should be written. Everyone might decide that a recount of the visit would be the best way of describing what happened. Children can then consider the elements of a recount and list them: *who, what, where, when, why, what happened?* (events in order) and *how we felt*. They might then construct a rough plan for the writing.

When	Last Friday
Who	Mrs Osborne's class
What	Went to the fire station
Where	In Swindon
Why	To find out what happens when a fire-alarm goes off

The planning session might take up all the time available, and the plan can then be placed ready to use in the next session.

It may be that the class decides to write a story. Perhaps the Reception children have run out of big books, and they wondered if the Year 1 pupils could possibly write a story for them. Children would start by brainstorming the setting, characters and a broad outline of the plot. Before the next session starts they can be challenged to think of a really good beginning sentence.

During shared writing, the cycle of questioning, discussing, facilitating, writing, reflecting and reviewing is continued. The teacher draws on pupils' opinions to make decisions, including how to begin a sentence, how to spell a word, how a character should develop, what can be added as a complication or anything else that crops up as the writing progresses.

Questions are used not only to motivate contributions, but to guide thinking and discussion. For example, *'Do you think that Reception children will understand that sentence? It seems to be a bit long'* or *'I'm not sure if the boy would really want to do that, would he? What do you think?'*

Each shared writing session is only ten to fifteen minutes in length, so pupils and teacher alike are able to reflect on their efforts when they return to the text the next day. This in itself is a good learning experience, as experienced writers always return to a text after a space of time, to reflect on it and make changes or additions that are then seen to be necessary.

NOTE: *After shared writing, the completed piece of writing is shared with the intended audience and feedback is sought. This enhances pupils' view of writing as purposeful and audience-driven. Follow-up activities are rarely necessary. If the shared writing sessions reveal a particular weakness or need, then a modelled writing session focusing on that element may be planned. Generally, however, pupils move on to a guided writing session that focuses on the text form encountered in shared writing. A sequel of this sort capitalises on the learning of both modelled and shared writing, and continues the transfer of writing responsibility to the pupil.*

As with modelled writing, the text can be left on display or filed for reference. Many classes create their own big books, which are carefully bound and made available for reading. Often these class-written texts become a favourite source of independent reading for children.

Guided Writing

What is Guided Writing?

Guided writing is the name given to the range of ways in which pupils are supported as they write individually within the supportive context of the classroom. This may occur when children are placed in ability groups that share a common need, or when the class is operating as a whole. The teacher scaffolds the writing process by:

- providing a plan or writing framework;

- being available for an on-the-spot conference;

- presiding over a short, focused episode of collaborative peer brainstorming when an answer is sought to a particularly thorny problem;

- providing appropriate resources and reference materials and helping individuals to use them if necessary.

Why Use Guided Writing Strategies?

Moving from the support that is provided through whole class shared writing to independent writing is fraught with danger for many pupils. Having to produce a piece of writing individually is a marked shift in responsibility from the supportive context of shared writing. Guided writing – both in a formal and informal context – offers the opportunity for appropriate scaffolding of the task. It also ensures that there are frequent reference points for both teacher and pupils, so that each individual is able to write with confidence in the knowledge that help will be provided if needed and that a suitable framework is being used to ensure that the writing is on track. Guided writing:

- familiarises a pupil with the management of the writing process;
- teaches pupils to be active participants in writing conferences;
- enables pupils to think about writing as a means of individual expression;
- supports pupils as they try to put into practice and co-ordinate all that they are learning about words, sentences and texts;
- helps pupils to gain confidence as they see others wrestling with the same issues;
- provides a forum for pupils to discuss writing and the writing process;
- helps pupils build up a language to talk about writing;
- provides total support for EAL pupils confronted with the demands of written English.

When Do I Use Guided Writing?

After children have participated in a series of modelled and shared writing sessions, guided writing provides an ideal context in which individuals can apply their new understandings and skills. Guided writing focuses on a specific text form, which provides the major scaffold for individual attempts.

In some instances, pupils may have been taught a particular text form at some previous time, but may require consolidation and further practice. Informal guided writing enables teachers to offer carefully structured support to individuals within a group, while encouraging independence. This helps pupils to gain competency and confidence as they refine strategies and acquire more control over the text form and the concepts and conventions of writing.

How Do I Choose my Objective?

The *First Steps* Literacy Developmental Continuum helps teachers identify what children are currently doing as writers, and the Major Teaching Emphases linked to each element of writing suggest how children can best be supported and challenged to move further along the developmental pathway. The Programme of Teaching Objectives provides a structure of progression for the required range of work. By accessing these two documents, teachers are able to choose objectives that will meet the needs of their pupils. For example:

- *Literacy Developmental Continuum:* Early Phase Indicator 7 – uses a small range of familiar text forms; and 14 – experiments with words drawn from language experience activities, literature, media and oral language of peers and others

- *Literacy Developmental Continuum:* Early Phase Major Teaching Emphasis 7 – focus on purpose, audience, structure and organisation of simple text forms, e.g. procedures; and 14 – build personal and class word banks, focusing on theme words, descriptive words, etc

- *National Literacy Strategy Programme of Teaching Objectives:* Year 2, Term 1, Text Level 15, 16, 17, 18 – to write simple instructions, using models from reading to organise instructions sequentially, using diagrams and appropriate register; and Word Level 10 – new words from reading linked to particular topics to build individual collections of personal interest or significant words.

Are Pupils Grouped?

Pupils undertake guided reading as individuals working within a larger group. Groups can be chosen on the basis of need. This can occur where a number of pupils are ready to use a text form with a greater degree of independence than when participating in shared writing or on the basis of writing ability. It is also possible to conduct a guided writing session with the whole class when appropriate. Mixed ability groups allow the sharing of ways that skilled writers deal with issues, but may pose logistical problems. For example, if a whole class is writing an instructional text, some will compose much more quickly than others and if questions arise during the writing, subsequent discussion may not be relevant to all children. Such problems are not insurmountable, but need to be considered.

Informal guided writing does not generally require children to be grouped. Guidance, in whatever form, is more appropriately given to individuals and need not involve all the children.

Paired writing

Paired writing can be extremely successful and beneficial to both partners. Children either choose a writing partner or are allocated one by the teacher. Children undertake the task together, sharing both the planning and the writing. It may be a good idea to teach children to take turns, each writing one sentence, to ensure that the more confident child does not always hold the pencil. Children need to be taught to write collaboratively, but the end result more than justifies time spent in setting up the procedure. One typical interaction overheard by a teacher, went like this:

Child 1: *How do you spell 'leap'?*
Child 2: *I'm not sure. Sound it out – l-ee-p.*
Child 1: *It doesn't look right.*
Child 2: *I know – it was in the book on frogs. I know just where it was. I'll find it... There you are – l-e-a-p.*
Child 1: *That looks right now. Thanks.*

This sample dialogue also provides an example of how a teaching objective such as Year 2, Term 1, Text Level 9 is implemented: 'through guided writing to apply phonological, graphic knowledge and sight vocabulary to spell words accurately'.

What Resources will I Need?

Pupils involved in guided writing simply need access to writing resources such as examples of text forms, class-generated frameworks and class-constructed word banks. Writing products from modelled and shared writing sessions are valuable references for pupils.

What is my Role?

In guided writing, the teacher's role is one of:

- supporting pupils in a wide variety of ways;
- providing constructive comments and posing key questions both during the writing process and when a draft is finished;
- modelling how to offer and receive constructive criticism;
- selecting pivotal points at which to provide assistance;
- pairing children appropriately when writing partners are needed

How Does Guided Writing Work?

Formal guided writing sessions have a clear sequence and structure. They begin when the teacher explains the purpose and audience for the writing.

Before Writing
Discussion Guide

Objective	Sample dialogue
Year 2, Term 1, Text Level 15,16, 17, 18 *(summary)*: To write simple instructions, using models from reading to organise instructions sequentially, using diagrams and appropriate register; and Word Level 10: New words from reading linked to particular topics to build individual collections of personal interest or significant words.	Teacher: *In this guided writing session we are going to write a procedure. Who can remember what a procedure is?* Pupil 1: *It's a list of instructions.* Teacher: *That's right. Do you remember, I wrote a procedure in modelled writing when I wrote down the recipe for chocolate crackles? We put it on the wall over there, so that we could use it in cooking. Then we all wrote a procedure in shared writing when we wrote the instructions for our new language game. We put that on the table beside the game. Can anybody remember how we start a procedure?* Pupil 2: *First of all we write the goal.* Teacher: *Well done. Yes, we state what it is we are aiming to do. Then what?* Pupil 3: *We make a list of things we'll need.* Teacher: *Good. After that?*

Objective	Sample dialogue
	Pupil 4: *We write a list of steps that we need to take, one after the other. Sometimes we draw something to show how you do it.* Pupil 5: *Then we wrote a sentence about what it should be like when you finish.* Teacher: *Excellent. You really do remember how to write a procedure.* Pupil 6: *Anyway, we made a chart, didn't we, with everything on it. Look – it's on the wall over there.* Teacher: *Yes, we created a framework to guide us after we had read several procedures other people had written. So there's lots of help around the room if you need it. The procedure we're going to write today is instructions about how to make a mask. We've been making masks in Art and Craft, so we all know exactly what to do. Yesterday Miss Burt came into our classroom and saw what we'd been doing. She was so impressed that she wants her children to make masks too. So she asked me if we would write down the instructions for her children. I thought that if we all did it, then every child next door could have their own set of instructions to follow. Let's just talk through what we did as we made the masks... If you feel you have forgotten any details, you can get a mask and remember each step you took as you look at it. Don't forget that you can illustrate your instructions if you think it will make it easier for the other children. Today I think we'll work with a partner... Now that each pair has found a good spot and you've got all you need, let's begin;...*

After making the purpose and audience clear, each invitation to write is preceded by a revision of the text form and an indication of available resources. Then it is wise to walk children through each step so that the actual procedure is fresh in their minds. Pupils need to be able to approach the task confidently, knowing that they are familiar with the form, that they understand the content and that they know where to go to for help should this be required. At reasonably short intervals, the teacher can invite one or two children to share what they have written up to that point.

During Writing
Discussion Guide

Objective	Sample dialogue
Year 2, Term 1, Text Level 15, 16, 17, 18 *(summary)*: To write simple instructions, using models from reading to organise instructions sequentially, using diagrams and appropriate register; Word Level 10: New words from reading linked to particular topics to build individual collections of personal interest or significant words; Text Level 9: Through guided writing to apply phonological, graphic knowledge and sight vocabulary to spell words accurately.	Teacher: *Who would like to read their opening statement?* Pupil 1: *Me. 'Making a Mask. I am going to tell you how to make an animal mask.'* Teacher: *That's a good title and opening statement. Anyone else?* Pupil 2: *I will. 'How to Make a Mask. You can have fun making a mask to act in a play.'* Pupil 3: *'Making Masks. Instructions for Making Masks.' Sam and I didn't know how to spell 'instructions', so we went to the chart on the wall and copied it.* Teacher: *That was a good thing to do. Well, we've had some excellent beginning statements, now let's write the next section. Remember, the next section tells the children what they are going to need. If you can't spell a word, be as resourceful as Sam and Mehru and try to find it for yourselves before you ask me. 'Instructions' was a very hard word to spell, and it was clever of those two to think of using it. Perhaps people would like to write it in their Word Books? I'll certainly add it to our class wall bank of interesting words.*

The cycle of rehearse, write, share, reflect, revise, share and rehearse continues, with the text being written in manageable chunks. These chunks could be paragraphs in a story. In an information text, the text structure often lends itself to chunking, as it does in a procedure.

Not every writer needs to share, and decisions about the writing remain with the author(s). Each pupil, or pair of pupils, is writing an individual text, but insights about how the text is structured and how problems are resolved will benefit the whole group.

Discussion Guide

Objective	Sample dialogue
Year 2, Term 1, Text Level 9: Through guided writing to apply phonological, graphic knowledge and sight vocabulary to spell words accurately. Sentence Level 6: To use a variety of simple organisational devices, e.g. arrows, lines, boxes, keys, to indicate sequences and relationships. Year 2, Term 1, Text Level 15, 16, 17, 18 (summary): To write simple instructions, using models from reading to organise instructions sequentially, using diagrams and appropriate register.	Teacher: *Can we stop for a minute and ask someone to read out their list of requirements?* Pupil 1: *'You need a big brown paper bag, a red balloon, a paper plate, straws, and a bottle top.'* Pupil 2: *What about scissors, glue and paints?* Pupil 3: *And a paint brush and a glue brush.* Teacher: *Goodness me, I didn't know we had used so many things. I should think that between us we've remembered everything. Well done. Now, can somebody tell me how you set out your list of requirements?* Pupil 4: *We put ours into a long list, because we thought it would be easier to check off.* Pupil 5: *We put ours in a box to make it stand out.* Pupil 6: *We just did ours one after the other, because we thought it would take up less space.* Pupil 7: *We were having our turn on the computer and we used a different font because we liked it.* Teacher: *Did anyone solve any spelling problems?* Pupil 8: *We couldn't remember whether there was one 'l' or two in 'balloon'. We wrote it down to see which looked right, but we still didn't know. We couldn't think where it might be written – it wasn't in our own list or the class bank, so we found it in the dictionary.* Teacher: *You **have** done well.* Pupil 9: *We sounded-out 'straws'. Str-aws.*

Objective	Sample dialogue
	Pupil 10: *We tried to spell 'scissors' without the 'c', but it looked funny, so we found the label on the jar on the art and craft table.* Pupil 11: *We thought it would be good if people knew what things were for, so we drew a picture of the mask and labelled all the bits with words and arrows.* Teacher: *I'm really looking forward to reading all your procedures before they go next door. I'm sure everyone will want to see what everybody else has done, there are so many good ideas being shared already! Now we'll start on the next section, which is the series of steps. Don't worry if you're not quite there yet, just take your time and don't rush. For those people who are ready to start writing the steps, are you happy about starting, or would you like us to talk about the steps again?*

After Writing

After the session is over, children share their products with the class and receive feedback. It is important that pupils are taught to offer positive feedback that encourages others. The simple framework of Two Stars and a Wish can be introduced to help pupils do this. Children are taught to make two comments about how well another pupil has achieved the objective, and a suggestion for a small improvement that could be made next time, such as:

Two Stars and a Wish

I really liked the drawings, which show exactly what you are expected to do.

I thought that the headings you used made it very easy to read.

It might help if the requirements were all in a box, so they stand out a little more.

Classmate: _____   Date _____

The reflection time that follows a guided writing session is extremely important. It is used to:

- support children as they think about whether the objectives of the session were achieved;
- reflect on *how* the objectives were achieved;
- talk about any additional learning that has taken place;
- discuss how such learning can be recorded and used in the future;
- think about the ways in which writing partners were able to help each other (in paired writing sessions)
- ensure that children know that their written products will be used for the purpose for which they were intended.

The teacher may then want to make a few organisational decisions.

- Should this session be continued the next day, so that writers have more time to proof read, edit, enhance, decorate or illustrate their scripts?
- Should these pieces of writing be considered first drafts or can they be used as final copies? Sometimes making young children rewrite a first draft can have a negative effect. Children often put a great deal of effort into their presentation, making drawings and decorating borders. Even if they have been advised not to do this, the temptation often proves irresistible. They are not only daunted by the thought of having to repeat the process, but they can also be extremely hurt by realising that a teacher thinks that it is necessary for them to do so! Redrafting a piece of writing may be a more appropriate activity for more mature writers, or for co-operative group working as in shared writing sessions.
- Should existing writing partnerships be continued as they are proving to be productive and positive, or would children benefit from a change of partner?

Guided writing sessions include a range of practices used to support and guide pupils as they write.

- Pupils work in pairs, sometimes because two children are similar in ability, and sometimes giving a weaker child the benefit of working with a more able partner.
- Structured plans and timelines are provided to enable children to participate in brief, but frequent 'conferences'. These reassure pupils that they are on the right track and bolster their use of appropriate strategies and skills.
- Frameworks and guiding questions are provided to prompt a writer's knowledge of a text type or strategy.
- Easily accessible resource material is provided and children are made aware that they can use it when they need to.

Independent Writing

Daily Writing

Children need to be given the opportunity for at least 10 to 15 minutes of uninterrupted writing each day. This may take place in the Literacy Hour, but is more likely to occur in lessons for other subject areas in which the text form is appropriate. It is through independent writing that many understandings about the written language are developed and extended. This has a profound effect on the reading as well as the writing understandings and competencies of children.

Daily writing provides excellent opportunities for enabling children to have the regular practice they need in applying the concepts, conventions and strategies they have learned in modelled and shared writing. It can also be used to encourage children to take risks and try out ideas, thus developing understandings in a non-threatening environment.

Language Experience

Teachers often use a shared experience as the basis for 'language experience' writing. For instance, the class may have been taken on an educational visit, participated in a local festival or seen a puppet show or play. Pupils talk about the experience, re-live aspects of it, think about the new insights they have gained and use the vocabulary they have learned in context before writing about the experience.

Language experience writing can be conducted as an independent activity, or it can form the basis of a modelled, shared or guided writing session. It makes connections between an experience the child has had, oral language and a written recount.

In recounting an experience to a group, and in translating an oral to a written text, and then re-reading it, a young child has the opportunity to:

- develop understandings about concepts and conventions of print;
- gradually build an awareness of the functions of words, letters and punctuation;
- come to terms with simple sentence structure;
- make connections between life experiences and oral and written language.

In the very early years, the teacher acts as scribe, writing down exactly what a child says. The text is entirely owned by the child, which is why this strategy is included as an independent function. Children help to make decisions about the use of written conventions.

The telling of an experience can stem from an individual child, or can be the result of a class activity or outing. When every child is involved, it is more appropriate to use the context of shared writing to retell and write down the experience.

Important features of language experience include:

- planning events that will interest the children and motivate them to recount and write them down;
- seizing the opportunity when a spontaneous event – like a mechanical digger excavating a trench outside the classroom – allows a teacher to capitalise on the natural, enthusiastic oral and written language of the children;
- allowing children to control the writing as far as they are able;
- publishing the finished product attractively to encourage personal re-readings (some classes make big books of language experience events which become sought-after reading for the whole class);
- using the published copy for additional reading activities.

Writing – Section 3

| **Written Conversation** |

Written conversation is a powerful tool that teachers can use in the early years of school. The teacher circulates as children are doing their daily writing and now and again writes comments or questions on a child's page that focus entirely on the meaning of the child's writing. This is quite different from the sort of comment or correction that is sometimes written down by teachers. Children love it when they have a real response from their teacher to what they are writing. One small boy was disappointed because his teacher had not written anything on his page for some days (she was recovering from flu). She arrived at his table one day to find that he had written *'I'm not writing no more until you write me back.'* She did!

Children appreciate a personal response to their writing from their teacher.

The power of this strategy lies in the fact that children can see that their teacher is genuinely interested in what they have to say. This motivates them to write more. Furthermore the teacher is able to reflect back to the writer the correct grammar and spelling without in any way 'correcting' the writing. Children eagerly read what the teacher has written and very often take note of spellings or conventions used in the adult version.

| **Word Processing** |

Very young children love using a word processor as much as older pupils. Many children are able to write their names efficiently in this way, long before they come to school, if they have access to a computer at home.

Computers are often used in schools to publish finished drafts, but if this is the only thing that happens, a great deal of the impact of a word processor is lost. Children do not need to learn to type before they start – they can pick out the letters for themselves and easily learn simple editing skills. Children are not afraid of technology, as adults often are, and will fearlessly approach a new challenge with enthusiasm and gain a great deal of satisfaction from the finished result. It does not matter in the least if the result is unorthodox! If a school has access to touch-sensitive boards, or concept keyboards, these can also be invaluable tools for independent writing. E-mail can be more problematic, as there is no guarantee that recipients will be able to read a child's message.

Message Boards

Start a message board in the classroom. A large piece of laminated card can be re-used many times. Children need little encouragement to write a message on the board. One child who had recently arrived from Italy wrote the following message: NO HATTA NO PLAYA. (The real thing cannot be reproduced as it was written on a white board.) A school rule had just been introduced which said that all children were to wear sun hats in the playground.

Sharing Circle

Children are encouraged to join a sharing circle where they can discuss their writing problems or share their triumphs. Initially, they need explicit guidance in the conduct of these sessions. The group sits in a circle and one child reads his or her writing aloud. Other group members listen and give feedback or ask questions. It is a good idea to teach the Two Stars and a Wish technique for giving feedback, as described on page 105, as this prevents negativity and maintains a positive climate. An example could be:

Two Stars and a Wish

It made me sad when you were writing about your old dog. I knew just how you felt and you wrote it beautifully.

I loved the bit where you tell about your new puppy.

I think the last sentence was a bit too long. Could you make it into two sentences?

Classmate: _____   Date _____

It can be useful at times to have a focus for sharing sessions, e.g. *'This week we are thinking about descriptions. Let's see if we can paint pictures in words for our audience, so that they can "see" what we are writing about.'* In this way children can focus on one small aspect of writing instead of being overwhelmed by trying to respond to everything at once.

Writer's Notebooks

If teachers talk about the ways in which authors of books collect ideas and words that catch their fancy and write them down in their own special notebooks, children will become very keen to do the same thing. Children then come to realise that writing is not always a grand production, but very often starts from something that is intimate and personal. If children wish to, they can share their writer's notes in a sharing circle, but they should never feel obliged to do so, as their notebooks are their own and their privacy should be respected. Children need to know that their notebooks are their own and that they can use them in any way they wish. Even small children are capable of writing a word or two, or of drawing something that they would like to write about later.

Children can:

- carry a small notebook in which they can record things they see that attract them;
- record feelings;
- jot down anything they have read that has special appeal;
- write down any tips people give them about writing;
- write down ideas they have that they can share with others;
- write down any emotive, interesting or descriptive words they might like to use in the future;
- draw something that will trigger a desire to write later on.

Lucky Bear and the Writing Bag

One day a teacher, who was working in a school serving a vast and problem-ridden housing estate, brought her beautiful teddy bear to school to show the children. They were entranced and named him Lucky Bear! She decided to take the idea further and provided Lucky Bear with a little back-pack. In the back-pack was Teddy's journal – an attractive exercise book covered with teddy bear wrapping paper. With the journal was a collection of attractive pencils and pens – some tiny, some huge, some with tassels on, and some with fancy erasers.

The children took it in turns to take Lucky Bear home on a Friday night. The idea was to give him a good time so that he could write about it in his journal. Some children read him stories, others took him to McDonalds for tea, and others took him to the shops or for a walk. He went to football matches, to church fetes, to barbecues and to gym lessons. The one thing he always did was to write about his exploits in his journal. A proud child would come to school on Monday morning, eager to read aloud to the class what Lucky Bear had written.

Several mothers, keen to let the teacher know what her family had done for Lucky Bear, wrote their own notes in the journal. The teacher had been very careful to explain to all the carers that each child must write exactly what he or she wanted in the journal, without correction or help. Adults conscientiously obeyed this rule, but did not want to be left out. In the end the teacher put another little notebook in the bag so that parents and carers could add their contributions. Many adults started to drop in to the school to make sure that their children were not forgetting a single detail of Lucky Bear's weekend adventures. Before long, Lucky Bear was joined by six cousins. None of them was ever lost. One had his hair cut by a younger sibling, and sometimes a teddy would return to school somewhat greasy, but none the worse for it.

A colleague, puzzled by the unusual sight of adults accompanying their children to school on Monday mornings, introduced a Lucky Lion to her class...

CONCLUSION

Modelled, shared and guided reading and writing provide a bridge from supportive, explicit reading and writing contexts to the demands of independent reading and writing. Children are privy to the prereading and prewriting, during reading and writing, and after reading and writing behaviours of a skilled reader and writer – the teacher.

Frequent discussion, held at strategic points when children are reading silently or out loud, focuses on the strategies employed in the quest for meaning. Frequent discussion points structured at specific intervals during the writing of a text focus on text form, grammatical structures and use of words and on the strategies children need to use as they write.

Paired reading or writing can be extremely beneficial for all children, as they share strategies and insights with each other. Guided reading and writing helps readers and writers take the final step towards full independence with confidence.

Modelled, shared and guided reading and writing are springboards for further highly focused teaching and learning. They can all be followed up by appropriate activities that help children consolidate, practise and extend what they have learned. These activities can be found in the other books in this series.

Reading and writing support and inform each other. The following table shows the natural flow from one context to another. This flow can occur in a small way in the context of one lesson. It can also occur over an extended period of time. These contexts for teaching need to be used frequently, cyclically and recurrently to ensure that children gain confidence and competence in the reading and writing of each text form. The teaching and learning process takes the form of an upward spiral, rather than the flat sequence that is implied by the table, as each revisiting of a process leads to further learning and enhanced understandings.

Aim	Reading Objective	Writing Objective
The aim of reading to children is to share the joy of reading with them.	Reading to children has as its sole objective to share the joy of books with children. There should be no hidden agenda.	
The aim of modelled reading or writing is to demonstrate the expert at work, reading or writing purposefully, fluently and reflectively.	**Modelled reading** is used to: • familiarise children with the structure and features of a text form • provide an explicit demonstration of the reading process and reading strategies • build children's knowledge of the English language • show how reading and writing are related • show how comprehension is shaped by a reader's experience of life • demonstrate the importance of reading as a means of deriving pleasure and learning • provide EAL children with access to the reading process and the intonation patterns of a fluent reader. *Modelled reading can be used before or after a modelled writing session.* *Control of the reading process lies entirely with the teacher.*	**Modelled writing** is used to: • build children's knowledge about the structure and features of a text form • provide explicit demonstrations of writing strategies and the writing process • build children's knowledge about the English language • show how reading and writing are related • show how writing can be shaped for different purposes and different audiences • demonstrate the importance of writing as a means of communication • enable EAL children to access the writing process without stress or anxiety, and to see how English is structured and written. *Modelled writing can be used before or after a modelled reading session.* *Control of the writing process lies entirely with the teacher.*

Conclusion – Section 4

Aim	Reading Objective	Writing Objective
The aim of shared reading and writing is to teach children to read and write through active participation in the processes involved, within a totally supportive and unthreatening context.	**Shared reading** enables children to: • access and enjoy a text that may be slightly beyond their independent reading level • increase fluency through the supported re-reading of a text • test their theories about reading in a safe and supportive environment • consolidate a sight vocabulary and knowledge of sound/letter relationships in an authentic context • gain insight into and experiment with decoding and comprehension strategies used by able readers • gain an understanding of sentence patterns and linguistic structures used by authors in a range of different text forms • build up a language to talk about and reflect on reading, discussing factors that make an effective and fluent reader • experience total support, e.g. when EAL pupils are confronted with the demands of reading English texts. *Shared reading can be used before or after a modelled reading or writing or a shared writing session.* *Control of the reading process is shared between pupils and the teacher.*	**Shared writing** enables children to: • participate in the writing of a text that may be slightly beyond their independent writing level • increase competency in the use of appropriate writing strategies, applying and consolidating new learning in a safe and supportive environment • spell some words automatically and develop understandings about the English spelling system • learn how competent writers use planning, proof reading and editing strategies and practise the use of these strategies • gain an understanding of sentence patterns and linguistic structures used by writers in a range of different text forms • build up a language to talk about and reflect on writing, discussing and evaluating what makes an effective and fluent writer • experience total support, e.g. when EAL pupils are confronted with the demands of written English. *Shared writing can be used before or after a modelled reading or writing or a shared reading session.* *Control of the reading process is shared between pupils and the teacher.*

Aim	Reading Objective	Writing Objective
The aim of guided reading and writing is to give children a structured and supported opportunity to read and write independently, putting into practice what they have been learning in modelled and shared reading and writing sessions.	**Guided reading** enables children to: • use their reading skills independently, but in a supportive session with direct guidance • compare their interpretations of text with others • practise strategies for making meaning at Word, Sentence and Text Levels • read silently and think critically with guidance and support from the teacher and other children • learn to monitor and reflect on their own reading • co-ordinate and internalise reading strategies and develop an effective understanding of the reading process. *Guided reading can be used after a modelled or shared reading session.* *Control of the reading process lies with individual pupils who receive on-going support from the teacher.*	**Guided writing** enables children to: • gain practise in the management of the writing process by writing with guidance and support • think about writing as a means of individual expression • put into practice all they have learned at the Word, Sentence and Text Levels • take part in contextualised discussion and gain support from other children wrestling with similar issues • learn to monitor and reflect on their own writing • co-ordinate and internalise writing strategies and develop an effective understanding of the writing process. *Guided writing can be used after a modelled or shared writing session.* *Control of the writing process lies with individual pupils who receive on-going support from a shared framework and from the teacher.*

Aim	Reading Objective	Writing Objective
The aim of independent reading and writing is to give children as many opportunities as possible to practise and consolidate their skills; make and learn from their own mistakes; and develop strong self-images of themselves as purposeful and effective readers and writers.	**Independent reading** enables children to: • practise the knowledge, skills and understandings they are learning • select texts and read for enjoyment and also to acquire knowledge • re-read texts they have worked on in teaching sessions • co-ordinate and refine strategies they have been taught • enhance their self-images as readers. *Independent reading can and should occur at any time.* *Control lies with individual pupils, who may wish to discuss issues afterwards.*	**Independent writing** enables children to: • practise the knowledge, skills and understandings they are learning • write for specific purposes, including self-actualisation and self-expression • take risks, try out ideas and further develop understandings and skills • co-ordinate and refine strategies they have been learning • enhance their self-images as writers. *Independent writing can and should occur at any time.* *Control lies with individual pupils who may receive feedback afterwards.*

Although the teaching of reading and writing has been separated into different contexts, children learn a great deal about reading through writing, and conversely learn a great deal about writing through reading.

Word identification knowledge supports spelling, just as spelling knowledge illuminates word identification. Nevertheless, children need to have explicit understandings in each area fed back into both the reading and writing processes to ensure that generalisation takes place.

SAMPLE LESSON PLANS

The following two sample lesson plans are intended to highlight the following applications of modelled, shared and guided reading and writing sessions.

- Modelled, shared and guided reading and writing sessions are clearly the teaching strategies chosen to 'drive' a literacy lesson. Although both have potential in working with texts in other subject areas, these strategies need to be considered within the context of this critical daily teaching period.

- Modelled, shared and guided reading and writing sessions relate to each other in purpose and/or content. This link has already been discussed earlier in this book. These sample lessons aim to illustrate how a chosen objective drives not only the teaching during these sessions, but also provides the focus for all subsequent activity within a literacy lesson. The objective, introduced and taught in the modelled or shared reading or writing component of the Literacy Hour, is consolidated and extended through relevant activities and through guided reading or writing with small groups. Discussion about progress towards the achievement of the objective then becomes the focus of the class reflection at the end of the session.

- Shared reading sessions are maximised in value when they are planned in a series. Pupils reap the benefit of rereading, which consolidates sight vocabulary and subject-specific word knowledge. Furthermore, beyond the first reading, pupils are able to increasingly shift their focus from decoding to comprehension and metacognition – that is, thinking about, and reflecting on, their own reading processes. Guided reading sessions, on the other hand, show how different groups might be matched to different texts to cater for differences in reading development. What will remain consistent across the week will be a weekly focus on a particular text type. This will enable pupils to consolidate understandings about the features of a text type, and to compare different examples of the same text type.

- The sample lesson plans demonstrate that the small group activities chosen have a clear and deliberate link to the preceding shared and/or guided reading sessions. Such activities are intended to balance the need for pupils to read and write daily, and to consider Text, Sentence and Word Level factors on a regular basis.

- Grouping pupils is a means to an end. By conducting shared reading sessions with mixed ability groups, teachers are promoting the sharing of interpretations of the text and strategies for making sense of it. Weaker readers benefit from the explicit demonstrations of proficient readers, particularly – but not only – the teacher. Guided reading sessions are normally organised in ability groups to enable pupils to be challenged by a text matched to their reading ability. The onus is on the pupil to read fluently and silently, so discussion can focus primarily on the comprehension of the text. How many groups are used and how they are arranged will depend on what the teacher is setting out to achieve. The social skills of the pupils and the classroom management skills of the teacher will be pivotal factors. The following sample lesson plans show a variety of grouping alternatives to assist teachers in making informed and useful choices.

Sample Lesson Plans – Section 5

Key Stage 1, Year 1, Term 2

(These lessons were adapted from plans written by Rebecca Wright Davidson.)
This sequence of two Literacy Hour lessons demonstrates the use of shared reading and modelled writing within the framework of the Literacy Hour to meet NLS Key Stage 1, Year 1, Term 1 Objectives.

Monday
Objectives

Pupils should be taught:

Text Level: 17	to use the term 'non-fiction', noting some specific features of a report, e.g. layout, titles
Sentence Level: 2	to decipher new or unfamiliar words by reading on, leaving a gap, then re-reading, using grammatical, contextual and phonic knowledge
Text Level: 2	(word focus) to use phonological, contextual, grammatical and graphic knowledge to work out, predict and check unknown words and to make sense of what they read

Shared Context

Shared Reading *15 minutes*
Sample text: *Whale Watching* by Josephine Croser, Heinemann, 1995

Before Reading
- Briefly discuss author, illustrator, title and cover, and the fact that the book is non-fiction. Discuss the difference between fiction and non-fiction.
- Briefly activate children's existing knowledge about whales by asking questions such as *'Tell me some things that you know about whales'*, and by inviting comments and predictions.
- Provide any useful background knowledge. For instance, whales are migratory (explain). Briefly refer to a map and explain their movements around oceans. This may include showing a few of the illustrations of Antarctica included in the text.
- Talk about and examine the layout of the book, including headings, maps, pictures etc.
- Clearly state the purpose for reading:
  1 Enjoyment and interest.
  2 Practising the read on, leave a gap and re-read strategy for identifying unknown words, then checking by using sense and sounding out.

During Reading
- Read the text aloud to the pupils. Include a few demonstrations of the use of the reading strategy discussed. Do not reduce interest in the text by stopping too often, but use sufficient demonstrations on which to base the 'after reading' discussion about 'Things Effective Readers Do.' For example, the teacher may hesitate over 'Antarctica', re-read to establish the sense, look at the picture and guess 'Arctic', then go back to the word and use syllabification An/tarc/tic/a to read it correctly. Mark where any reading strategies are modelled with a small sticky note in the margin. In this way the flow of the reading is not interrupted but the point of error can be returned to easily during the 'after reading' discussion.
- Draw attention to structural and organisational features as they occur and show how they help readers to comprehend text.
- Model enjoyment and genuine responses.

After Reading
- Discuss the strategies that the pupils saw the teacher use while reading. Return to the sections marked with the sticky note(s) and talk explicitly about the thinking involved. *'Do you remember when I was reading this line? I read "Perhaps it has been to the Arctic" instead of "Antarctica". I thought it was "Arctic" because of the snow and ice in the illustrations. I felt confused and realised something wasn't right so I went back and sounded out the syllables – An/tarc/tic/a. That's how I was able to read the word Antarctica correctly.'* Repeat the strategy of thinking aloud to explain other instances when the reading strategy was used.
- Explain that the things you did to identify words when reading are things that all effective readers do and that all pupils need to learn to do. Say that you will make a chart to remind pupils of the strategies they can use when reading.

Shared Context Word/Sentence Level Focus

Modelled Writing
- Using the information volunteered by the children before reading *Whale Watching*, as well as the knowledge gained from the text, model the writing of the class's own whale text, in abbreviated point form. Use headings to provide structure, e.g. appearance, habitat, food, reproduction.
- Discuss and chart interesting and previously unknown words. You might wish to discuss words that have a *w* and *wh* in them, but you may feel that this would be too much for the children to absorb in one lesson.
- The modelled writing text will now be used for the group tasks so that pupils have a text which they can read successfully, in order to practise and apply the strategy they are learning. Although the text is written in front of the pupils it will have been devised in advance.

Interesting Word Focus
What Comes Next? Choose a word from the text that starts with *w* or *wh*, e.g. waves, wonder, where, whale, why, when.

Group Tasks	
Group A **Pupils and teacher working together**	**Group B** **Word Level & Sentence Level** **Pupils working independently**
Guided Reading *Before reading* Together, begin to generate a strip chart entitled 'Things we can do to help us read'. A strip chart consists of a large piece of backing paper onto which sentence strips are pasted, see Appendix 2 page 132. The chart should include strategies that pupils are aware that they or other effective readers use while reading. The chart is gradually built up over time. *During reading* The teacher then conducts the guided reading session, using focus questions that help children extract literal, inferential and evaluative meaning from the text. If the group is able to, they can read *Baleen Whales* (see Tuesday's lesson plan). If the reading ability of the group is low, they can read the text that was constructed in modelled writing. Children should be encouraged to use the chart they have made to remind them of what to do if they can not read a word. *After reading* Discuss how children are using the read on, leave a gap, predict and reread strategy, supported by sounding-out, contextual and visual knowledge. Encourage children to discuss facts about whales, comparing what they knew with what they have found out.	**Sentence Reconstruction** *Groups 1 and 2 (able readers)* 1. Pupils work in pairs. Each partner has one of the two prepared sentences that have just been modelled. Photocopy the sentences onto different coloured paper so that the partners don't get the words of their sentences mixed up. 2. Pupils read their sentences to each other and then cut up their sentences, mixing up the words. Children then reconstruct their own sentences and check them against the text. Children can then swap sentences and repeat the process. 3. Children paste or copy their reconstructed sentences into their work book ready for the sharing session and for the teacher to check. *Groups 3 and 4 (less able readers)* These children may only reconstruct one sentence instead of two or three sentences or the whole text. If a group is very weak, it can be given the additional support of a copy of the text to help them with their reconstruction.

Whole Class Sharing – Plenary session
Group A: One child explains the chart that the group has begun and suggests how readers can use it. A few more children use relevant sections of the text to explain how they applied the strategies when they were reading, just as the teacher did in the first session. For instance: *'When I was reading* Whale Watching *to Keira, I didn't know what this word said,'* (showing the word mountain) *'so I thought about the ideas on our chart and it reminded me to look at the picture and look at the first letter. I read on and then I knew it said mountains.'* *Group B:* Children talk about how they managed to put their sentences together. The teacher encourages children to say that they needed to stop and think about the sentences, and sometimes re-read them, to see if they made sense. They could tell if a word was right if the sentence made sense. The teacher then invites some children to comment about: • tricky parts and how they solved their problem • something they have learnt, e.g. how to read a new word. The teacher compares the way in which children made sense of their jumbled sentences with the way readers make sense of a sentence that has an unknown word in it. Refer back to the objectives of the lesson and talk about how they have been achieved. Inform children that tomorrow's shared reading is also about whales.
Assessment • Were children able to identify some features of a non-fiction text? What do they need to revise? • Were children able to use meaning, grammatical knowledge and visual cues to identify words and reconstruct sentences?

Tuesday

Objectives
Pupils should be taught:

Text Level: 17	to use the term 'non-fiction', noting some specific features of a report, e.g. layout, titles
Sentence Level: 2	to decipher new or unfamiliar words by reading on, leaving a gap, then re-reading, using grammatical, contextual and phonic knowledge
Text Level: 2	(word focus) to use phonological, contextual, grammatical and graphic knowledge to work out, predict and check unknown words and to make sense of what they read
Word Level: 3	to discriminate and read words with initial consonant clusters
Word Level: 10	collect new words from reading and make collections of personal interest or significant words linked to particular topics

Shared Context

Shared Reading *15 minutes*
Sample text: *Baleen Whales* by J. Croser, Heinemann, 1992

Before Reading
- Briefly discuss author, illustrator, title and cover, comparing this with yesterday's book.
- Reactivate children's existing knowledge about whales and recall any relevant points from yesterday's reading and discussion.
- Clearly state the purpose for reading:
  1. Enjoyment and furthering interest in whales.
  2. Consciously using reading strategies learned and discussed yesterday (refer to strip chart constructed by guided reading group).

During Reading
- Read the text aloud to the pupils. Include a few demonstrations of the use of the read on, leave a gap and reread strategy, in combination with use of phonics, contextual understanding and grammatical sense. Reinforce some of the strategies used yesterday. Mark the point of any modelled reading strategies with a small note in the margin. In this way the flow of the reading is not interrupted but the point of error can be returned to easily after reading.
- Comment on any new facts that surface, or any difference in structure and presentation of the text.
- Model interest, enjoyment and genuine responses.

After Reading
- Discuss the strategies that the pupils saw the teacher use while reading. Return to the sections marked with the sticky note(s) and explicitly talk about the thinking involved e.g. *'Do you remember when I was reading this line? I worked out what this word said by...'* The strategy used will be added to Group A's chart during the follow up activity if it has not already been listed.

Shared Context Word/Sentence Level Focus

Modelled Writing

Briefly discuss newly-acquired whale information and then use this to create a modelled writing text. Focus on and discuss words that have a *w* and *wh* in them. The modelled writing text will be used in the following group tasks to provide pupils with a text which they can read successfully and use to practise and apply the strategies they are learning. Although the text seems to the children to be spontaneously generated, it has actually been constructed beforehand.

Interesting Word Focus   *3 minutes*

Briefly conduct a Sound Sleuth activity to find all the words beginning with *w* from either *Whale Watching* or *Baleen Whales,* e.g. waves, wonder, where, whale, why, when... Categorise the words according to the presence or absence of an *h*. Chart words.

Group Tasks	
Group A **Pupils and teacher working together**	**Group B** **Word Level & Sentence Level** **Pupils working independently**
Guided Reading *Before reading* Start the session by adding any additional strategies noticed by the children in the shared reading session. Children and teacher work with the *Baleen Whales* text or the modelled writing text. Encourage children to practise and apply the strategies listed on their chart. Work with the children to devise a focus question for the first segment of text. Make sure that this question will ensure that children make an inference. *During reading* Talk about the strategies the children are using and encourage them to demonstrate their use of a specific strategy to each other. Discuss the contributions offered by the children. Encourage children to substantiate their answers by reading the relevant portion of text. Devise the next question. *After reading* Talk about what children have discovered and ask them to substantiate what they say. Continue to discuss their use of strategies and praise them for being able to think and talk about how they read.	**Word Sorting** *Groups 1 and 2 (able readers)* Children look through copies of the text, finding any words that start with initial consonant clusters. These are written onto small cards and placed in a pile in the middle of the table. Children then sort the words into matching sets of consonant clusters. Children then think of as many other words as they can that start with the same clusters and add them to their pile. These words can then be used in future Word Sorts games. *Groups 3 and 4 (less able readers)* These children are given a pile of words on small cards, already prepared by the teacher, starting with a range of consonant clusters, drawn from today's text. They sort them into piles of like clusters. They then think of as many words as they can that start in the same way and add them to the pile.

Sample Lesson Plans – Section 5

Whole Class Sharing – Plenary session

Group A: One child explains the additions to the chart. A few more children use relevant sections of the text to demonstrate and then explain how they applied the strategies when they were reading, just as the teacher did in the first session. For instance: *'When I was reading* Baleen Whales *this part didn't make sense. So I had to re-read it and then I understood it.'* Remaining children tell the others about finding and sorting words with initial consonant clusters and explain how the sorting activity will help them to read similar words more easily when they meet them next time.

Assessment
- How much did the children remember about the structure and features of non-fiction texts from the previous day, and were they able to apply their knowledge?
- Were the children able to use the reading strategy they were learning effectively?
- What other strategies were they able to use successfully?
- Did children recognise consonant clusters? Were they able to read these words easily? Could they begin to generalise their knowledge?

APPENDIX 1 – SCOPE AND SEQUENCE CHART

Key: E – Exposure, T – Teaching, M – Maintenance

Punctuation		R	Yrs 1-2	3-4	5-6
	Full Stops				
	use of full stops to end statements, e.g. Writing is fun.	E/T	T	M	M
	use of full stops in initials, e.g. W.D. Murphy.	E	E	T	M
	use of full stops in abbreviations (those that do not end in the final letter of the word), e.g. Mon., Dec., Sec.	E	E	T	M
	N.B. Full stops are not required after titles, dates (unless at the end of a sentence), measurement symbols and abbreviations that end with the final letter of the word.				
	Capital Letters				
	use of capital letters to begin sentences, e.g. Writing takes time.	E/T	T	M	M
	use of capital letters for proper nouns (names, days, months, places, titles, streets), e.g. Susan, Tuesday, February, France, Captain Cook, Victoria Street.	E/T	E	T	M
	use of capital letters for adjectives derived from proper nouns, e.g. French.	E/T	E	M	M
	use of capital letters for the pronoun I.	E	T	M	M
	use of capital letters for book titles, first word in a line of poetry, e.g. Gulliver's Travels, Slowly the river rises.	E/T	E	T	M
	use of capital letters for emphasis, e.g. HAPPY BIRTHDAY!	E	T	M	M
	use of capital letters for names of deity, special days, names of institutions, e.g. *God*, *Boxing Day*, *Brunswick Primary School*.	E	T	M	M
	N.B. Capital letters are not necessary for points of the compass (unless forming part of a title) and seasons of the year.				
	Question Marks				
	use of question marks at the end of sentences that ask for information, e.g. Why are we doing this?	E/T	T	M	M
	N.B. Question marks are not needed: (i) when using indirect speech, e.g. The captain was asked if he was fit to play. (ii) when a sentence is a request, e.g. Can you hurry up.				
	Exclamation Marks				
	use of exclamation marks to show strong feeling, e.g. What a mess!	E/T	T	T	M

Appendix 1 – Scope and Sequence Chart

	R	Yrs 1-2	3-4	5-6
Commas				
use of commas:				
to separate items in a series, e.g. They collected shells, driftwood, coral and cuttlefish.	E	E/T	M	M
N.B. The items may be nouns, verbs, adjectives or groups of words.				
to separate a word/words used in a sentence for further explanation, e.g. Mary, the golden-haired girl, won the medal.		E	T	T
before joining words when they join two main clauses, e.g. He wanted to travel to China, but he wanted to learn the language first.			E	T
to separate main and subordinate clauses, e.g. When they heard the final siren, the players leapt into the air.		E	T	M
to separate the person spoken to from the rest of the sentence, e.g. Richard, mind the wet paint.		E	T	M
after words like *yes* and *no*, e.g. No, you can't come in here.		E	T	M
to separate month and year in date, e.g. Sunday, June 27, 1999.		E	T	M
to follow signal words at the beginning of sentences, e.g. However, I believe …			E	T
Apostrophes				
use of apostrophes for contractions, e.g. can't, won't doesn't.	E	T	M	M
use of apostrophes to show ownership, e.g. Barry's holiday, elephants' enclosure.		E	T	M
use of apostrophes to indicate letters or numbers omitted, e.g. 'phone, o'clock, '99.		E	T	M
N.B. Apostrophes are not necessary when the noun is descriptive rather than possessive, e.g. boys club, infants school.				
Quotation Marks				
use of quotation marks when using direct speech, e.g *"That will do!"* she shouted.	E	T	T	M
N.B. Quotation marks are not used for indirect speech, e.g. Brewhouse told his players to run harder and share the ball.				
use of quotation marks to show quotations within quotations, e.g. *"My father always said* 'look on the bright side' *and I suppose I do,"* explained Dennis.				E
use of quotation marks before and after titles or words used in an unorthodox manner, e.g. Some viewers actually consider "The Video Show" a form of "entertainment".			E	T

Appendix 1 – Scope and Sequence Chart

	R	Yrs 1-2	3-4	5-6
Colon				
use of colons to:				
introduce a list, e.g. Greg packed his drawing gear: pencils, paints, crayons, paper and easel.				E/T
introduce a quotation, e.g. The boss said: "I have some good news for you."				E/T
introduce an explanation, summary or elaboration of the first half of sentence, e.g. I'm not much of a runner: I tend to cross the pain barrier just getting out of bed.				E/T
Semi-colon				
use of semi-colons to:				
join sentences with two or more main clauses, e.g. A face appeared at the window; he was one determined animal.			E	E
separate clauses containing commas, e.g. At that point our captain, who had previously remained calm, lost control and stormed off; the game had to be abandoned.			E	E
Hyphen				
use of hyphens to:				
join some parts of compound words, e.g. father-in-law, heavy-handed.			E	T
join a group of words to form an expression, e.g. good-for-nothing.			E	T
write numbers and fractions that consist of more than one word, e.g. five-sixths, forty-nine.			E	T
Dash				
use of a dash to:				
introduce a list, e.g. The burglar collected his tools – torch, screwdriver, saw and tyre lever.			E	T
create surprise, e.g. She pulled herself to her feet – still prepared to fight.			E	T

Use of Sentences

	R	Yrs 1-2	3-4	5-6
Write Sentences				
write sentences containing a main verb, e.g. The child *hit* the ball.	E/T	M	M	M
N.B. Verbs are often called 'doing words' because they describe an action. To make sense a sentence must have a verb.				
Join Sentences				
join sentences using conjuctions, e.g. *and, then, but, because, so, yet, or.*	E	T	M	M

Appendix 1 – Scope and Sequence Chart

		R	Yrs 1-2	3-4	5-6
Modification of Sentences	use of adjectives to enhance the meaning of sentences, e.g. The *little* girl hit the *white* ball.	E	T	M	M
	N.B. An adjective tells you more about a noun or pronoun. Adjectives are frequently referred to as "describing words".				
	use of adverbs to enhance the meaning of sentences, e.g. The child hit the ball *powerfully*.				
	N.B. An adverb provides more information about a verb, and sometimes adjectives and other adverbs. An adverb often answers the questions: How? When? or Why?		E	T	M
	demonstrate understanding of function of adjectives.		E	T	M
	define the term adjective.		E	T	M
	demonstrate understanding of function of adverbs.		E	T	M
	define the term adverb.		E	T	M
	identify and use adjectival phrases, e.g. The child *with the strong muscles* hit the ball.			E	T
	N.B. A phrase is a group of words which is unable to make sense on its own because it does not contain a verb. Adjectival phrases takes the place of adjectives.				
	identify and use adverbial phrases, e.g. The child hit the ball to *first base*. Adverbial phrases act as adverbs.			E	T
	identify and use adjectival clauses, e.g. The child hit the ball *which was thrown by the bowler*.			E	E/T
	N.B. A clause is a group of words which includes a verb. A main clause can stand independently as a sentence, however a subordinate clause (shown above) relies on a main clause for its meaning. An adjectival clause serves as an adjective in a sentence.				
	identify and use adverbial clauses, e.g. The child hit the ball *because he was angry*. An adverbial clause acts as an adverb.				E/T
	Isolate Subject and Predicate				
	isolate subject and predicate in a sentence, e.g. *The huge bird* flew over the fence.			E	T
	N.B. The subject is the thing or person featured in the sentence, while the predicate is what is said about the subject.				
	write sentences in which the subject and verb agree in number, e.g. A *packet* of lollies *was* on the table. A *box* of matches *is* small. *The children were* visiting the zoo.				E/T

Appendix 1 – Scope and Sequence Chart

Parts of Speech		R	Yrs 1-2	3-4	5-6
	Use of Pronouns				
	write pronouns which are consistent with the number and case of the subject or object to which these pronouns refer, i.e. subject-pronoun agreement, e.g. *The children* watched the game, *They* enjoyed it.		E	T	M
	N.B. Pronouns are words referring to a person or thing, e.g. *them, him*.				
	write an appropriate pronoun for a previously stated subject or object in order to avoid repetition, e.g. *My Dad* walked into the shop. *He* bought a packet of lollies. The car ran into *the* people. An ambulance took *them* to hospital.	E	T	M	M
	Adverbs in Sentences				
	explain functions of adjectives, nouns, verbs and adverbs in sentences, e.g. The large bird flew gracefully.	E	T	M	M
	Avoid Repetition				
	write vivid adjectives and explicit nouns to avoid unnecessary repetition or pronouns, e.g. *The lion sprang at the hunter. The angry beast growled horribly. It clawed the man viciously.*	E	T	M	M
	not				
	The lion sprang at the hunter. *It growled. It clawed ...*				
	Avoid Redundancies				
	e.g. My Dad *he* ..., The train was *more* bigger ...	E	T	M	M
	Structure of Text				
	Make alterations:				
	add words to enhance meaning.	T	M	M	M
	change words to achieve exact description.	E	T	M	M
	delete words to tighten sentences.	E	T	M	M
	re-arrange words to produce a more convincing order.		E	T	M
	add phrases to enhance meaning of sentences.	E	T	M	M
	re-arrange sentences to produce a more convincing sequence.		E	T	M
	write paragraphs appropriate to the structure of the form.		E	T	M
	re-arrange paragraphs to produce a more convincing order.				E

Adapted from: *Programming Ideas K-7,* Volume 5 (1985) Ministry of Education, Western Australia.

APPENDIX 2 – WORD IDENTIFICATION STRATEGIES

This chart is intended only as a guide and not as something to be displayed in a classroom. It should be built up gradually by children as they learn about different strategies in modelled and shared reading and then practise them in guided reading.

Things we can do to help us read

When we come to a word we don't know, we can:

Sound out the letters.

Think about the letter pattern in case it could be sounded in a different way.

Divide it into syllables.

Look at the picture, if there is one.

Read the sentence, leave a gap, and see if we can guess what word would make sense.

GLOSSARY

active voice – the subject of the verb carries out some action, e.g. *The child drew a picture*

adjectival clause – a clause used to describe a noun or pronoun, e.g. The man *who was carrying an umbrella,* walked past my house

adjectival phrase – a phrase used to describe a noun or pronoun, e.g. The boy *with long legs* won the race

adjective – a word used to describe a noun or pronoun, e.g. He was a *fat* cat

adverb – a word that modifies or more clearly defines the action of a verb, e.g. The boy ran *quickly*

adverbial clause – a clause which modifies or more clearly defines the action of a verb, e.g. The boy ran quickly, *thinking he would miss the train*

adverbial phrase – a phrase which modifies or more clearly defines the action of a verb, e.g. 'The boy ran quickly, *his bag in his hand ...*'

affix – a word used to describe both prefixes and suffixes

alliteration – the repetition of initial sounds in successive words, e.g. *The wind whistled wildly*

anecdotes – a report or description of an observed behaviour

annotation – textual comment in a book which may be written in a margin

apostrophes – a punctuation mark to indicate a *contraction* or *possession*. *contraction:* The apostrophe replaces omitted letter or letters, e.g. *hadn't*. *possession:* applied to all single or collective noun possessives (except *its*) – the apostrophe is added before the s which indicates ownership: e.g. *John's book; the cat's tail*. For a plural marked by an s, the apostrophe is added after the s: e.g. *cats' tails; girls' hats*.

article – a grammatical marker linked to a noun; may be definite *(the);* or indefinite *(a* and *an)*

assessment – gathering data to better understand the skills, knowledge and behaviours of a learner

auditory texts – text that is heard read aloud

blends – the sounds of two or more letters joined with minimal changes in those sounds, e.g. *st* in *stick*

characterisation – how an author presents a character in speech, action or reaction from other characters

choral reading – the synchronised reading aloud of a common text by two or more people

clause – a group of words within a sentence containing a subject and a verb, e.g. The man *who was wearing a hat,* boarded the train

cloze procedure – instructional strategy involving the completion of incomplete sentences, phrases or clauses

colon – punctuation mark denoting a long pause when speaking, used before a list or to begin a further explanation

compound word – a word as a single unit of meaning but consisting of two separate words, e.g. *buttonhole, football*

concepts of print – recognition that print needs to be arranged in an orderly fashion for effective communication

conjunction – a connecting word, joining words, phrases, clauses and sentences, e.g. *because, and, but, however*

consonant – all letters of the alphabet except *a,e,i,o,u*

context – the cultural or social situation in which language occurs. This may be verbal or non-verbal language

contextual cues – information which comes from both the text, and the reader's interpretation of the text, that helps identify a word or group of words

contextualisation – keeping literacy in the broad linguistic, social and psychological experience of the learner so that response to text is possible

continua – more than one continuum

Glossary

continuum – a systematic, continuously structured table of identified skills, behaviours and understandings which increase in complexity

contraction – a word which represents a shortened version of one or two other words. Letters are omitted and substituted with an apostrophe, e.g. *did not* becomes *didn't*

conventions of print – rules that govern the customary use of print in literacy

criteria – principles taken as standards of judgment

critical literacy – analysis of the values and beliefs conveyed in a text

cueing systems – any of the various sources of information that may help a reader comprehend a text, e.g. using semantic, syntactic and graphophonic knowledge, pictures, diagrams, background knowledge

cumulative rhyme – a rhyme with many details repeated until it reaches a climax

deconstruction – dismantling a text section by section, to reveal its structure and linguistic features

developmental – changes in the complexity and organisation of behaviour related to growth over time

diagnostic tools – instruments for the assessment of skills, knowledge and behaviours of a learner

dialogue – conversation between two or more people

digraphs – two letters that together represent one sound, e.g. *ch, ck, ai*

Directed Reading Activities (DRA) – step-by-step instruction involving clearly defined purposes for reading and directed questions

directionality – the orientation of English print from left to right and top to bottom

drafting – writing in a rough form. It may be edited later for publication

editing – clarifying meaning at the sentence level

element – a component part, e.g. in literacy: *reading and writing*

embedded – set in a context that makes sense to the reader

evaluative – a level of comprehension involving judgement beyond the text based on background knowledge brought to the text

explanation – form of text which makes facts or situations known in detail

exposition – forms of argumentative or persuasive text

fiction – imaginative narrative in any form

figurative language – language enriched by figures of speech and images created by words, e.g. *The ghostly trees bent close to the ground*

fluency – the ability to read or write language smoothly, easily or readily

form – structure of particular genre

grammar – fundamental pattern of a dialect. The way words are combined to make meaning

graphic organisers (concept maps) – structures or tables that enable a reader to visualise, record and retrieve information from a text

graphophonic – sound-symbol relationship often called 'phonics'

guided reading – a small group, directed reading activity in which the teacher guides comprehension of the text

homonym – a word with the same oral or written form as another, but with different meanings, e.g. *bear (animal); bear (tolerate)*

homophone – a word which sounds the same as another, but which is spelt differently, e.g. *stare, stair*

implicit – a meaning, intended, but not directly stated by an author

indicator – evidence, from gathered data, of acquired skills, knowledge or behaviours used to direct teaching

inferential – a level of comprehension related to understanding implied in the text but not directly stated

inflectional endings – an ending which, when added to a word, changes its form but not the class of word, e.g. *stop, stopped; dress, dresses*

informational text – see non-fiction texts

interactive – communication either between two or more persons or persons interacting with media, e.g. *book, computer*

interjection – exclamation sometimes formed by actual words or sounds indicating emotional noises, e.g. *Oh! Phew! Gosh!*

intonation pattern – vocal pitch that contributes to the meaning of spoken phrases, e.g. *Shut the door. SHUT THE DOOR! Shut the door? SHUT THE DOOR!!*
Intonation is used to convey meaning, e.g. sarcasm, questioning, humour

learning journey – personally presenting a report of the products of learning, reflecting skills, knowledge and understanding acquired in that learning, e.g. *taking a visitor on a learning journey around the classroom*

linguistic feature – a language feature of a text type which makes it recognisable, e.g. *grammatical patterns, layout* and *style*

literal meaning – meaning clearly stated in text or in speech

logograph – an orthographic symbol that represents one or more words, e.g. *a pictograph; a symbol ☎ for telephone*

medial vowel – referring to the middle vowel used in a word, e.g. *'u' in cup*

metaphor – an expression in which one idea is described in terms of another, e.g. *the road was a ribbon of moonlight*

miscue analysis – a formal examination of oral reading using running records as a basis for analysing language skills of pupils

mnemonic – technique to assist with remembering something, e.g. *an invented sentence using initial letters of each word to remember a sequence of facts, such as notes on a keyboard* or *a verse to assist in remembering correct spelling such as 'The principal is my pal.'*

modelled writing – teaching the writing process by example and 'thinking out aloud'

modelling – serving as an example of a learner by 'thinking out aloud' and reflecting on learning processes

monitor – to continue to observe learning behaviours, skills, knowledge and understanding

morpheme – the smallest meaningful unit of a word, e.g. *'un', 'reason'* and *'able'* in the word *'unreasonable'*

morphology – the study of the structure of words

narrative – a story expressed orally or in writing

nominalisation – a process is turned into a thing, e.g. *It was announced today that we won the competition* becomes *Our winning of the competition was announced today*

non-fiction – text designed to explain or describe rather than entertain – *see also* **informational text**

noun – a name of a person, place, object, emotion etc.

onset – as in 'onset and rime': the part of a syllable before the 'nucleus': usually any consonants which precede the vowel, e.g. *'tr' in 'trick'*

orientation – usually the beginning passage of a text. Providing the reader with enough background information to comprehend the text from the writer's perspective

outcomes – effectiveness of a plan or teaching or learning

paragraph – begins with a new line. Used to organise thoughts. A section of a piece of writing used to change focus of time, place or speaker

participle – parts of a verb. Participles help form the tenses of the verb

passive voice – a sentence in which the subject of the verb receives an action instead of carrying it out, e.g. *The man was hit by the car*

personification – a figure or speech giving 'human-like' qualities to animals, ideas, things, e.g. *The moon smiled down upon us*

phase – a stage of development

phoneme – the smallest unit of sound in a word, e.g. *'b' as in 'book'*

phonemic awareness – the awareness of the sounds or phonemes that make up spoken words

phonic awareness (see also **graphophonic**) – an awareness of the sound-symbol relationship used in words

phonics – a way of teaching which stresses sound-symbol relationships

Glossary

phonological awareness – the awareness of the sounds that make up words in learning to read or spell

phrase – a small group of words, which is not a complete sentence because it has no verb

plural – a word which represents more than one, e.g. *trees, roses, sheep, women*

portfolio – a collection of pupil's work to evaluate learning progress

predicate – what is said about the subject in a sentence

prefix – part of a word which is the small addition of one or more letters at the beginning of a base word, e.g. *un* in *unhappy*

prepositions – words which show the relationship of one thing to another, e.g. The boy chased his dog *under* the barn

procedure – form of text conveying how to do something

pronoun – a word which stands instead of a noun, e.g. The boy looked for his dog because *it* had run away

proof reading – final check of punctuation and spelling

punctuation – graphic marks used to help readers clarify meaning of written text

recount – a form of text which tells an event in detail

reflection – the process of consciously thinking over acquired skills, knowledge and understanding

report (as a noun) – form of text which is an official or formal account of something

report (as a verb) – presenting an account of something to another

revision – changes made to ideas at the whole text and paragraph level

rime – as in onset and rime: a vowel and any following consonants of a syllable, e.g. *ick* in the word *trick*

root – the meaningful bases of words, e.g. *'aqua'* in *'aquatic'* meaning *water*

rote learning – acquiring new knowledge through repetitive drill

rubric – a scoring device which explicitly states criteria on which judgements are made about quality, understanding and demonstrated proficiency

scaffolding – the provision of structured support which enables pupils to focus on a specific objective by removing the need to deal with peripheral features

scanning – quickly reading material to locate a specific detail such as a name, date or place

segmentation of words – breaking down the components of a word into phonemes, e.g. *ch-ur-ch; c-a-t*

semi-colon – a punctuation mark which joins two parts of a sentence or separates sentence parts in a list, e.g. *The bicycle was broken; its wheel was twisted*

sentence – *simple* – a sentence with one clause, e.g. *Sam hit me*
       compound – a sentence made up of simple sentences joined by conjuctions, e.g. *Sam hit me but I didn't cry*
       complex – a sentence containing a main clause and a subordinate clause, e.g. *I didn't cry when Sam hit me because I wanted to be brave*

semantic cue – information from the meaning of a text or root word, that aids in the identification of an unknown word

shared reading – an instructional strategy where the teacher involves a group of children in text reading for the purpose of modelling reading behaviours

shared writing – an instructional strategy where the teacher involves a group of children in the writing of a text for the purpose of modelling writing behaviours

sight vocabulary – words which are automatically identified

signal phrases – phrases which indicate relationships between parts of sentences. These may include time order, cause and effect, comparison or extra information, e.g. *in the meantime, because of this*

simile – a simile compares two things, referring to a likeness between them, e.g. *He was shaking like a leaf.* Words which are commonly used in a simile are: *as, like, as though, as if* etc.

skimming – reading quickly to gain a general impression of the main idea of a text

sociogram – diagrammatical representation of the relationships between characters

standard English – the accepted form of language for education, government and business
stereotype – a perception based on culturally dominant ideas
strategy – a method employed to improve or modify performance of a task
subject – the subject is a noun or a pronoun of which the sentence is all about
sub-vocalises – moves lips and mouth during silent reading
suffix – a word part added to the end of a base word that changes the meaning of the word, e.g. *en* in the word *oxen*
syllabification – the division of words into syllables, e.g. *won/der/ful*
syntactic cue – knowledge of the grammar and sentence patterns of language used when reading
syntax – the study of how sentences are formed and the pattern and structure of word order and grammar
teaching emphasis – a planning focus or goal for teaching
tense – used to show the time at which the action of a verb takes place, e.g. present tense: *stay*, past tense: *stayed*, future tense: *will stay*
text – spoken or written linguistic communication
text form – also known as **text type** – a category of text with particular structural and language features, e.g. *narrative, limerick, argument, report*
text innovation – the practice of making changes to text
topic sentence – a lead sentence containing the main idea of a paragraph
Venn diagram – overlapping circles that demonstrate elements of subsets that are unique to the subset or common to both
verb – a word which defines an action or a state of being, e.g. *run, walk, imagine, become, sing*
vocabulary – words of language used by a person or group
word derivation – using an affix to change a base word, e.g. *predict – prediction; sign – signature*
working memory (sometimes called **M space**) – the number of discrete elements that the mind can cope with at one time
zone of proximal development (as defined by **Vygotsky**) – the distance between a learner's actual development and potential development through problem solving and support

BIBLIOGRAPHY

ADAMS M. 1990, *Beginning to Read: Thinking and Learning About Print*, 'A Bradford Book', The MIT Press, Cambridge, Massachusetts.

BARRATT-PUGH C. and ROHL M., *Learning to Read and Write*, Allen and Unwin, Sydney, Australia (in press).

BEAN W and BOUFFLER C. 1986, *Spell by Writing*, Primary English Teaching Association (PETA), Rozelle, NSW, Australia.

BRICE-HEATH S. 1983, *Ways With Words: Language, Life and Work in Communities and Classrooms*, Cambridge University Press, Cambridge.

BROCKHOFF V. 1995, Learning Journeys, *Practically Primary*, Volume 1, pp6-11. Australian Literacy Educators Association (ALEA), Victoria, Australia.

BROWNE H. and MATHIE V. 1990, *Inside Whole Language: A Classroom View*, Primary English Teaching Association, Sydney, Australia.

BRUINSMA R. 1990, 'Learning to ride a bike and learning to read: Children's Conception of Reading', *The Australian Journal of Reading*, Volume 13, No2.

BRUNER J. 1986, *Actual Minds, Possible Worlds*, Harvard University Press, Massachusetts.

BUTLER A. and TURNBILL J. 1984, *Towards a Reading, Writing Classroom*, Primary English Teaching Association (PETA), Rozelle, NSW, Australia.

CAMBOURNE B. 1988, *The Whole Story*, Ashton Scholastic, Aukland, New Zealand.

CASE R. 1985, *Intellectual Development, Birth to Adulthood*, Academic Press Inc. London.

CHAMBERS A. 1993, *Tell Me – Children reading and talk*, Thimble Press, Gloucester.

CHRISTIE F. and ROTHERY J. 1989, *Writing in Schools, Reader*, Deakin University Press, Geelong, VIC, Australia.

CLAY M. 1987, 'Implementing Reading Recovery: Systematic Adaptations to an Education Innovation', *New Zealand Journal of Educational Studies* 22 (1).

COLLERSON J. 1988, *Writing for Life*, Primary English Teaching Association (PETA), Rozelle, NSW, Australia.

CUMMINS J. 1984, *Bilingualism and Special Education, Issues in Assessment and Pedagogy, Multilingual Matters*, Clevedon, Avon.

DAVEY B. 1983, '"Think Aloud" – Modelling the cognitive processes of reading comprehension'. *Journal of Reading*, 27 (1).

DEREWIANKA B. 1990, *Exploring How Texts Work*, Primary English Teaching Association (PETA), Rozelle, NSW, Australia.

DONALDSON M. 1978, *Children's Minds*, William Collins, Glasgow.

ECT 418 Language Studies, Children's Writing 1984, *Children's Writing: Study Guide*, Deakin University Press, Geelong, VIC, Australia.

ERICSON L. AND FRASER JULIEBO M. 1998, *The Phonological Awareness Handbook for Kindergarten and Primary Teachers*, International Reading Association, Delaware, USA.

FRANK M. 1979, *If you're trying to teach kids to write, you've just gotta have this book*, Incentive Publications, Nashville, Tennessee, USA.

FREEMAN Y.S. AND D.E. 1998, *ESL/EFL Teaching: Principles for Success*, Heinemann, Portsmith, New Hampshire.

FURNISS, E. AND GREEN P. 1991, *The Literacy Agenda*, Eleanor Curtin Publishing, Melbourne, Australia.

GENTRY J.R. 1981, 'Learning To Spell Developmentally', *The Reading Teacher*, vol.34, no. 4, International Reading Association, Newark Delaware, USA.

GENTRY J.R. 1982, 'Spelling Genius at Work: An Analysis of Developmental Spelling in GYNS AT WRK', *The Reading Teacher*, vol 36, no. 2, International Reading Association, Newark Delaware, USA.

Gentry J.R. 1987, *Spel...is a Four Letter Word,* Ashton Scholastic, Gosford, NSW, Australia.

Goldsmith P. and Robinson R. (n.d.), *Developing Word Knowledge* (Pen Note 58), Primary English Teaching Association, Rozelle, NSW, Australia.

Graves D.H. 1981, *Writing: Teachers and Children at Work,* Heinemann Educational, Melbourne, Australia.

Greg L.W. and Steinberg I.R. 1980, *Cognitive Processes in Writing,* Lawrence Earlbaum Association, New Jersey, USA.

Grieve R. and Hughes M. (eds) 1990, *Understanding Children,* Blackwell, Oxford.

Heenan J.E. 1986, *Writing Process and Product,* Longman Paul Ltd, Auckland, NZ.

Henderson E.H. and Beers J.W. 1980, *Developmental and Cognitive Aspects of Learning to Spell,* International Reading Association, Newark, Delaware, USA.

Hill S. and Hill T. 1990, *The Collaborative Classroom,* Eleanor Curtain Publishing, Melbourne, VIC, Australia.

Holdaway D. 1972, *Independence in Reading. A handbook on individualised procedures,* Ashton Scholastic, Auckland, New Zealand.

Jenkins R. (ed.) 1986, *Spelling is Forever,* Australian Reading Association, Carlton South, VIC, Australia.

Johnston T.D. and Louis D.R. 1985, *Literacy Through Literature,* Methuen Australia, Melbourne, Australia.

Johnston T.D. 1988, *Unriddling the World,* Wesley Foundation for Research in Literacy Inc., South Perth, Australia. *(out of print)*

Kroll B.M. and Wells G. 1983, *Explorations in the Development of Writing Theory, Research and Practice,* Wiley, Chichester, UK.

Lahey M. 1988, *Language Disorders and Language Development,* Macmillan, New York.

Larson R.L. 1975, *Children and Writing in the Elementary School: Theories and Techniques,* Oxford University Press, Oxford, UK.

Leki I. 1992, *Understanding ESL Writers: A Guide for Teachers,* Boynton Cook Publishers Inc. Portsmith, New Hampshire.

Martin J.R. 1989, 'Technically and Abstraction: Language for Creation of Specialised Knowledge', Paper presented to Language in Education Conference, Macquarie University, NSW, Australia.

Martin J.R. and Rothery J. 1988, 'Classification and Framing: Double Dealing in a Pedagogic Discourse', paper presented to Post-World Reading Symposium: Language in Learning, University of Sydney, NSW, Australia.

Martin J.R. and Rothery J. 1986, *Exploring and Explaining: Factual Writing in the Primary School,* paper presented to ARA conference, Perth, Australia.

Martin J.R. and Rothery Joan 1986, 'Writing Report Project': *Working Papers in Linguistics No 4,* Linguistics Department, University of Sydney, NSW, Australia.

McCracken M.A. and McCracken R.J. 1979, *Reading, Writing and Language: A Practical Guide for Primary Teachers,* Peguis, Winnipeg, Canada.

Morris A. and Stewart-Dore N. *Learning to Learn from Text. Effective Reading in the Content Area,* Addison-Wesley, North Ryde, NSW, Australia.

New Zealand Ministry of Education. 1996, *Reading For Life,* Learning Media Limited, Wellington, New Zealand.

Palincsar A. 1984, *The Quest for Meaning from Expository Text: A Teacher Guided Journey.* 'Comprehension Instruction: Perspectives and Suggestions'. Duffy G., Roehler L and Mason J. Longman, New York.

Bibliography

Parkes B. 1990, *Stories to Tell Teacher's Book,* Oxford University Press, Melbourne, Australia.

Phinney M.Y. 1988, *Reading With the Troubled Reader,* Ashton Scholastic, NSW, Australia.

Perera K. 1984, *Children's Writing and Reading: Analysing classroom language,* Basil Blackwell, London.

Pressley M. and Harris K.R. 1990, 'What we really know about strategy instruction', *Educational Leadership,* September 1990, pp.31-34.

Publications Branch 1984, *Early Literacy Inservice Course,* Education Department of South Australia.

Raphael T. 1982, 'Question Answering Strategies For Children', *The Reading Teacher,* November 1982, pp185-90.

Rothery J. 1984, 'The Development of Genres – Primary to Junior Secondary School' in *Language Studies: Children Writing, Study Guide,* (ed) Deakin University Press.

Rowe C. and Lomas B. 1985, *Spell for Writing,* Oxford University Press, Melbourne, VIC, Australia.

Sloan P. and Latham R. 1989, *Teaching Frameworks,* paper presented to ARA Conference, Perth, Australia.

Stewart-Dore N. (ed) 1986, Writing and Reading to Learn, Primary English Teaching Association (PETA) Rozelle, NSW, Australia.

Temple C.A., Nathan R.G. and Burns N.A. 1982, *The Beginnings of Writing,* Allyn and Bacon Inc., Boston, Massachusetts, USA.

Tizard and Hughes 1984, *Young Children Learning: Talking and thinking at home and school,* Fontana, London.

Tough J. 1977, *Talking and Learning: A Guide for Fostering Communication Skills in Nursery and Infant Schools,* Ward Lock Educational for The Schools Council, London.

Vygotsky L.S. 1978, *Mind in Society The Development of Higher Psychological Processes,* (eds) Michael Cole, Vera John-Steiner, Sylvia Scribner, Ellen Souberman, Havard University Press, Cambridge, Mass.

Waters M. and Montgomery J. *Children's Writing Proposals,* Reading Around Series, Australian Reading Association, Melbourne, Australia.

Weaver C. 1988, *Reading Process and Practice: From socio-psycholinguistics to whole language,* Heinemann Books, Portsmith, New Hampshire USA.

Weaver C. 1996, *Teaching Grammar in Context,* Boynton/Cook Publishers, Portsmith, New Hampshire.

Weeks B. and Leaker J. 1991, *Managing Literacy Assessment with Young Learners,* Era Publications, Flinders Park, South Australia.

Wells C.G. 1986, *The Meaning Makers: Children Learning Language and Using Language to Learn,* Heinemann, Portsmith, New Hampshire.

Wells C.G. 1987, *'The language experience of five year old children at home and at school',* in Literacy, language and schooling, (ed) J. Cook-Gumperz, Heinemann, Exeter, New Hampshire.

Westerby C.E. 1985, 'Learning to talk – talking to learn: Oral-literate language differences', in *Communication skills and Classroom Success: Therapy methodologies for language-learning disabled pupils,* (ed) C.S. Simon, Taylor and Francis, London.

Westerby C.E. 1986, 'Learning to talk – talking to learn', in C. Simon, *Communication Skills and Classroom Success: Therapy methodology for language disabled studies,* College Hill Press, San Diego, California.

Wilkinson A., Barnsley G., Hanna P. and Swan M. 1980, *Assessing Language Development,* Oxford University Press, Oxford, UK.

UK BIBLIOGRAPHY

BEARD ROGER. (Ed) (1995), Rhyme, Reading and Writing, London, Hodder and Stoughton.

BEARNE EVE. (1995), Greater Expectations: Children Reading and Writing, London Cassell.

BROWN MAUDE AND WILLIAMS ALEX. (1995), Eager Readers: A Whole Language Approach to Literacy in the primary school through using big-books, Giant Steps but sole distribution by Madeleine Lindley Ltd. (this book has no ISBN).

BROWNE ANN. (1996), Developing Language and Literacy 3-8, London Paul Chapman Publishing.

CAMPBELL ROBIN. (1995), Reading in the early years handbook, Buckingham, Open University Press.

CARTER RONALD. (1995), Key Words in Language and Literacy, London, Routledge.

CLIPSON-BOYLES SUZI. (1996), Supporting Language and Literacy: A Handbook for Those Who Assist in Early Years Settings, London, David Fulton Publishers.

COLES M. AND HALL C. (1999), Children's Reading Choices, London, Routledge.

EDUCATION DEPARTMENT OF WESTERN AUSTRALIA. (1994), First Steps Worldwide Edition (in eight volumes) Melbourne, Rigby Heinemann.

EDWARDS VIV. (1996), Reading in Multilingual Classrooms, Reading, Reading and Language Information Centre.

ELLIS SUE AND BARRS MYRA. (Eds.) (1996), The Core Book: A Structured Approach to using Books within the Reading Curriculum, London, Centre for Language in Primary Education (CLPE).

FOUNTAS I.C. AND PINNELL G.S. (1966), Guided Reading: Good First Teaching for All Children, Portsmouth NH, Heinemann.

FOUNTAS I.C. AND PINNELL G.S. (1998), Word Matters: Teaching Phonics and Spelling in the Reading/Writing Classroom, Portsmouth NH, Heinemann.

GRAHAM JUDITH. (1997), Cracking Good Books: Teaching literature at Key Stage 2, Sheffield, NATE.

GRAHAM JUDITH AND KELLY ALISON. (Eds.) (1977), Reading Under Control: Teaching Reading in the Primary School, London, David Fulton, in association with Roehampton Institute.

HALL NIGEL AND ROBINSON ANNE. (1995), Exploring Writing and play in the early years, London, David Fulton Publishers.

MARRIOT STUART. (1995), Read On: Using fiction in the primary school, London, Paul Chapman Publishing.

MEEK MARGARET. (1996), Information and Book Learning, Stroud, Thimble Press.

MOORE MAGGIE AND WADE BARRIE. (1995), Supporting Readers: School and classroom strategies, London, David Fulton Publishers.

REES FELICITY. (Ed) (1997), The Writing Repertoire. Developing Writing at Key Stage 2, Slough, National Foundation for Educational Research.

SEALEY ALISON. (1996), Learning About Language: Issues for Primary Teachers, Buckingham, Open University Press.

WEINBERGER JO. (1996), Literacy Goes To School: The Parents' Role in Young Children's Literacy Learning, London, Paul Chapman Publishing.

WRAY DAVID AND LEWIS MAUREEN. (1997), Extending Literacy children reading and writing non-fiction, London, Routledge.

ACKNOWLEDGEMENTS

First Steps was conceived and developed by **Alison Dewsbury** for the Education Department of Western Australia. The project team worked under her direction.

The following people made major contributions to the original *First Steps* materials:

Bruce Shortland Jones of Curtin University of Technology and **Judith Rivalland** of Edith Cowan University both contributed original work and acted as Consultants to the *First Steps* Project.

Glenda Raison, then of the Education Department of Western Australia, constructed and wrote the *Writing Developmental Continuum.*

Judith Rivalland was responsible for the concept development and construction of the *Continua of Forms.* Supporting material was researched and written by **Glenda Raison** in consultation with **Judith Rivalland.**

Diana Rees, Education Department of Western Australia, wrote the *Spelling Continuum* in consultation with **Judith Rivalland.** Diana also wrote the section on *Spelling Journal* in the *Spelling Resource Book.* **Kay Kovalevs** wrote the *Graphophonic and Word Study* component of this book. Material from the *Spelling Room Notes* written by **Judith Rivalland** were included in this publication.

Diana Rees and **Bruce Shortland Jones** wrote the Reading Developmental Continuum. Diana wrote the chapter on *Children with Reading Difficulties.* **Glenda Raison** wrote the section on *Contexts for Reading.* Bruce Shortland Jones wrote the *Reading Comprehension* section. He also edited all the initial publications of *First Steps.*

Jennifer Evans, Education Department of Western Australia, researched, developed and wrote the *Oral Language Developmental Continuum and the Oral Language Continua of Forms.*

Leanne Allen, then Speech Pathologist Consultant for the Education and Health Departments of Western Australia researched, developed and wrote the *Oral Language Resource Book.*

Ross Bindon, Education Department of Western Australia, wrote the *Teaching Grammar* component of the *Writing Resource Book.* **Kay Kovalevs,** Education Department of Western Australia, wrote the *Problem Solving Approach to Teaching Writing* included in the same book.

The **Principal and Staff of Highgate Primary School,** supported by **Anna Sinclair,** Education Department of Western Australia and **Caroline Barratt-Pugh** of Edith Cowan University, Western Australia, were responsible for the components on teaching children for whom English is a second language. **Kay Kovalevs,** then Deputy Principal of Christmas Island District High School, also made invaluable contributions in this area.

Beverly Derewianka, Lecturer in Language Education at the University of Woollongong contributed the section on the features of non-fiction text forms.

Peter Sloan and **Ross Latham,** then of Edith Cowan University, Perth, Western Australia contributed sections on *Teaching Children How To Write Informational Texts.*

Terry D. Johnson, Professor of Education, Faculty of Education, University of Victoria, British Colombia, Canada made many generous contributions to the books.

Glenda Raison revised and reconstructed the *Writing Developmental Continuum* and *Resource Books* that were published by Longman Cheshire in 1994. **Alison Dewsbury** revised and reconstructed the *Spelling and Reading Continua* and *Resource Books* and wrote the introductory section of all the books for the Longman Cheshire edition.

Caroline Barratt-Pugh wrote the section on *Catering for Diversity* and working with children for whom English is a second language.

TITLES IN THIS SERIES

First Steps NLS Edition titles available are:

A practical introduction to First Steps
Assessment Teaching and Learning
ISBN 435 01441 2

How to assess children's literacy
Literacy Developmental Continuum
ISBN 435 01442 0

How to assess, plan and teach
Word and Sentence Work at Key Stage 1
ISBN 435 01443 9
Word and Sentence Work at Key Stage 2
ISBN 435 01444 7

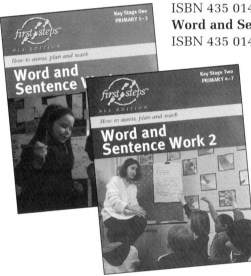

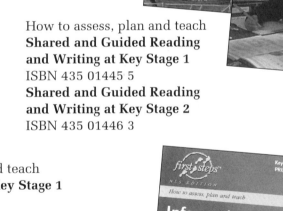

How to assess, plan and teach
Shared and Guided Reading and Writing at Key Stage 1
ISBN 435 01445 5
Shared and Guided Reading and Writing at Key Stage 2
ISBN 435 01446 3

How to assess, plan and teach
Fiction and Poetry at Key Stage 1
ISBN 435 01447 1
Fiction and Poetry at Key Stage 2
ISBN 435 01448 X

How to assess, plan and teach
Information Texts at Key Stage 1
ISBN 435 01449 8
Information Texts at Key Stage 2
ISBN 435 01450 1

To place your order please phone 01865 888020

FIRST STEPS PROFESSIONAL DEVELOPMENT

Teachers, literacy coordinators, heads, advisors and inspectors have all benefited from *First Steps* professional development courses.

First Steps professional development enables you to:

- Use all the developmental continuum to **assess** the literacy skills and understandings of ALL pupils
- Use this assessment to **select** developmentally appropriate teaching strategies and classroom activities to achieve medium and short term targets
- **Prepare teaching plans** for whole class and differentiated small groups at text, sentence and word level.

To support your literacy teaching further and to gain maximum benefit from your *First Steps* materials, we recommend you attend a *First Steps* professional development course. The *First Steps* books are an integral part of each workshop in the training.

First Steps Tutor Training Course

This five-day training course is suitable for all members of the teaching profession. Tutor training provides a detailed look at the teaching strategies and literacy content of *First Steps*. It prepares participants to present *First Steps* school-based training and to support whole school implementation based on school development plans.

Participants receive comprehensive presenter materials which include session outlines, overhead transparency masters, handouts and audio-visual materials to ensure school based training sessions run smoothly.

First Steps School-Based Training Course

This two-day traing course is suitable for a group of teachers in their own school. School-Based training focuses on *First Steps* approaches and teaching strategies that are the foundation of literacy teaching. The initial two-day course can be extended by the addition of day course options from the full selection of *First Steps* training days.

Contact GHPD on 01865 314630
to find out more about *First Steps*
training courses